Insight Phrase Book
Italian
Original text: Elisabeth Graf-Riemann
Editor: Sabine von Loeffelholz
English edition translated by: Paul Fletcher
Edited by: Renée Holler and Cathy Muscat

Managing Editor: Tony Halliday
Editorial Director: Brian Bell

CONTACTING THE EDITORS: As every effort is made to provide accurate information in this publication, we would appreciate it if readers would call our attention to any errors and omissions by contacting:
Apa Publications, PO Box 7910, London SE1 1WE, England.
Fax: (44 20) 7403 0290
e-mail: insight@apaguide.demon.co.uk

Information has been obtained from sources believed to be reliable, but its accuracy and completeness, and the opinions based thereon, are not guaranteed.

© 2000 APA Publications GmbH & Co. Verlag KG Singapore Branch, Singapore.

1st edition 2000

Printed in Singapore by Insight Print Services (Pte) Ltd

Original edition © Polyglott-Verlag Dr Bolte KG, Munich

Distributed in the UK & Ireland by:
GeoCenter International Ltd
The Viables Centre, Harrow Way, Basingstoke,
Hampshire RG22 4BJ
Tel: (44 1256) 817987, Fax: (44 1256) 817-988

Distributed in the United States by:
Langenscheidt Publishers, Inc.
46–35 54th Road, Maspeth, NY 11378
Tel: (1 718) 784-0055, Fax: (1 718) 784-0640

Worldwide distribution enquiries:
APA Publications GmbH & Co. Verlag KG (Singapore Branch)
38 Joo Koon Road, Singapore 628990
Tel: (65) 865-1600, Fax: (65) 861-6438

INSIGHT PHRASE BOOK

ITALIAN

Apa Publications

Contents

Introduction

About this book

Insight Phrase Books are the perfect companion when touring abroad as they cover all the everyday situations faced by travellers who are not familiar with the language of their holiday hosts.

The sentences and expressions translated here have been chosen carefully so that you can make yourself understood quickly and easily. You will not find any complicated sentence constructions or long word lists. Nearly all the sentences have been compiled from basic phrases so that by substituting words and other expressions, you will be able to cope with a variety of conversational situations.

The word lists at the end of each section are themed and this will make it easy for you to vary what you want to say. You will be able to make yourself understood quickly in Italian with the minimum vocabulary. You won't need to spend a long time searching for the word you want.

So that you can understand what others are saying to you in everyday situations, for example at the doctors, at the border, we have marked with an asterisk (*) those phrases and questions that you are likely to hear frequently.

The simplified pronunciation guide geared towards English speakers will help you to say correctly the words you need. You will also find a summary of basic pronunciation information, together with a brief introduction to Italian grammar.

This introduction is followed by nine chapters containing examples of sentences from general and tourist-related situations. You will find general tips and guidance not just in the chapter entitled *Practical Information*, but also elsewhere in the book. The various feature boxes contain useful information on such matters as meal times, using public transport and telephones, the different categories of hotels and restaurants and lots more.

At the end of the book you will find an English-Italian dictionary, which can be used for reference and as an index, the page number referring to an entry in one of the nine chapters. The Italian-English dictionary contains a selection of important words and abbreviations, which you are likely to encounter on signs, notices and information boards.

Hoping you have lots of fun on your travels, Buon viaggio! [bwon **vyaj**jo] *(Have a good trip!)*.

Pronunciation

All the Italian words included in this guide are given a phonetic rendering. This always appears in square brackets after the translation and there are no special symbols to remember.

You will see that where a word has more than one syllable, the stressed syllable is shown in bold, e.g. momento [mo**men**to] *(moment)*, tavolo [**ta**volo] *(table)*.

Italian is an easy and logical language to read and you will probably find yourself reading straight from the translation before long.

Although the phonetic rendering can be read as though it were English, the following points about pronunciation should be noted:

– **c** and **cc** when they precede the vowels a, o and u are pronounced as a k, e.g. camera [**ka**maira] *(room)*; coda [**ko**da] *(traffic jam)*. Before e and i as ch, e.g. cinque [**cheen**kway] *(five)*; centro [**chen**tro] *(centre)*.

– **ch** and **cch** are pronounced as k, e.g. che [kay] *(what)*; chiesa [**ky**ay**z**a] *(church)*.

– **ci** and **cci** when they precede the vowels a, o and u are pronounced as ch, e.g. ciao [chow] *(hi!)*; cioccolata [choko**lata**] *(chocolate)*.

– **g** before an a, o and u is a hard g like the English goal, e.g. ragazza [ra**gatz**a] *(girl)*; when followed by an e or an i, then it becomes a soft g like gentle, e.g. gente [**jen**tay] *(people)*; oggi [**oj**jee] *(today)*.

– **gh** is always pronounced like a g, e.g. funghi [**foon**gee] *(mushrooms)*.

– **gi** or **ggi** are pronounced as a soft g, e.g. mangiare [man**jar**ay] *(to eat)*; oggi [**oj**jee] *(today)*.

– **gl** makes an ly sound as in stallion, e.g. figlia [**feel**ya] *(daughter)*; moglie [**mol**yay] *(wife)*.

– **gn** sounds like ny as in onion, e.g. signora [seen**yor**a] *(woman)*; montagna [mon**tan**ya] *(mountain)*.

– the **h** is always silent, e.g. hai [**a**-ee] *([you] have)*; hotel [o**tel**] *(hotel)*.

– **qu** is a kw sound, e.g. acqua [**akw**a] *(water)*; quando [**kwan**do] *(when)*.

– the **r** is rolled, e.g. rosso [**ros**so] *(red)*.

– **sc** before a, o and u sounds like sk, e.g. scusa [**skoo**za] *(sorry)*; but before e and i as a sh sound, e.g. uscita [oo**shee**ta] *(exit)*.

– **sch** is always sk, e.g. pesche [**pes**kay] *(peaches)*; Ischia [**eesk**ya] *(Ischia)*.

– **sci** makes a sh sound when before a, o and u, e.g. lasciare [la**shar**ay] *(to leave)*.

When two or more vowels occur next to each other, then each vowel is heard, e.g. paese [pa-**ay**zay] *(country)*; europeo [ayooro**pay**o] *(European)*; cucchiaino [kookya-**ee**no] *(spoon)*; when an i occurs before a stressed vowel or between two vowels, then it is pronounced as a y,

e.g. escursione [eskoorsy**o**nay] *(excursion)*; lieve [**ly**ayvay] *(light)*.

Stress and accent

Generally speaking, it is the last but one syllable which is stressed when the word ends in a vowel, e.g. buon giorno [bwon⌣**jor**no] *(hello, good-day)*; turismo [too**ree**zmo] *(tourism)*; escursione [eskoorsy**o**nay] *(excursion)*.

If the stress occurs on a different syllable, then an accent shows the stressed syllable, e.g. perché [per**kay**] *(why)*; lui può [looee pwo] *(he can)*; nazionalità [natsyonalee**ta**] *(nationality)*; libertà [leebair**ta**] *(freedom)*.

The Italian alphabet

A a	[a]
B b	[bee]
C c	[chee]
D d	[dee]
E e	[eh]
F f	[**eff**ay]
G g	[jee]
H h	[**ak**ka]
I i	[ee]
J j	[ee **loon**go]
K k	[**kap**pa]
L l	[**el**lay]
M m	[**em**may]
N n	[**en**nay]
O o	[o]
P p	[pee]
Q q	[koo]
R r	[**er**ray]
S s	[**ess**ay]
T t	[tee]
U u	[oo]
V v	[vu]
W w	[vu **dop**pyo]
X x	[eex]
Y y	[**eep**seelon]
Z z	[**tzay**ta]

Italian Grammar In Brief

The article

In Italian all nouns are either masculine *[m]* or feminine *[f]*.

The definite article

Masculine singular: **il** and **lo**. Lo is shortened to l' before nouns that begin with a vowel:
il cane [eel **ka**nay] *(the dog);* lo sportello [lo spor**tel**lo] *(the booking office);* l'occhio [**lok**yo] *(the eye).*

Masculine plural: **i** and **gli**
i cani [ee **ka**nee] *(the dogs);* gli occhi; [lyee **ok**kee] *(the eyes).*

Feminine singular: **la**
la casa [la **ka**za] *(the house);* la scuola [la **skwo**la] *(the school).*

Feminine plural: **le**
le case [lay **ka**zay] *(the houses);* le scuole [lay **skwo**lay] *(the schools).*

Indefinite article

Masculine singular **un** and **uno**
un libro [oon **lee**bro] *(a book);* uno stivale [**oo**no stee**va**lay] *(a boot).*

The *plural* of the indefinite article is formed by the partitive article di and the plural form of the definite article **dei (di+i), degli (di+gli):**
dei libri [**day**ee **lee**bree] *(books);* degli stivali [**day**lyee stee**va**lee] *(boots).*

Feminine singular: **una**
una casa [**oo**na **ka**za] *(a house);* una barca [**oo**na **bar**ka] *(a boat).*

Feminine plural: **delle (di+le)**
delle case [**del**lay **ka**zay] *(houses);* delle barche [**del**lay **bar**kay] *(boats).*

Nouns

The gender of the noun in Italian can usually be established by the ending in its singular form. Masculine nouns usually end in -o, e.g. il libro [eel **lee**bro] *(the book);* feminine nouns in -a: la casa [la **ka**za] *(the house).*

There are a few exceptions to this rule, e.g. il telegramma [eel te**le**gram**ma] *(the telegram);* il problema [eel pro**blay**ma] *(the problem).*

Nouns ending in -e can be either masculine or feminine, e.g. la madre [la **ma**dray] *(the mother);* il padre [eel **pa**dray] *(the father).*

Forming plurals

Nouns ending in -a form the plural in -e: la mela [la **may**la] *(the apple)* – le mele [lay **may**lay] *(the apples).*

Nouns ending in -o form the plural in -i: il libro [il **lee**bro] *(the book)* – i libri [ee **lee**bree] *(the books).*

Adjectives

Most adjectives are like nouns and end in -o. They form the feminine plural with -a, plural with -e, e.g. buono/buona [**bwo**no/**bwo**na] *(good);* caro/cara [**ka**ro/**ka**ra] *(dear, expensive).*

Il vino buono [eel **vee**no **bwo**no] *(the good wine),* i vini buoni [ee **vee**nee **bwo**nee] *(the good wines);* la casa bella [la **ka**za **bel**la] *(the beautiful house),* le case belle [lay **ka**zay **bel**lay] *(the beautiful houses).*

The adjective always matches the gender and number of the noun, even when it is not next to the noun in the sentence, e.g. un libro bello [oon **lee**bro **bel**lo] *(a beautiful book);* Il libro è bello. [eel **lee**bro ay **bel**lo] *(The book is beautiful.)*

Adjectives ending in -e usually do not have their own feminine form, e.g. grande [**gran**day] *(large);* verde [**vair**day] *(green).*

Position of the adjective

The describing word usually goes next to the noun, e.g. la casa grande [la **ka**za granday] *(the large house)*; la città bella [la cheetta bella] *(the beautiful town).*

Some common adjectives such as molto [**mol**to] *(many)*, poco [**po**ko] *(few)* or buono [**bwo**no] *(good)* can go before the noun, e.g. Buon viaggio [bwon‿**vya**jjo] *(Have a good trip!)*

Comparison of adjectives

To create the comparative form of an adjective, Italian uses più [pyoo] *(more)*, e.g. caro [**ka**ro] *(expensive)*, più caro [pyoo **ka**ro] *(more expensive)*. For the superlative form, the definite article is required, e.g. il più caro [eel pyoo **ka**ro] *(the most expensive)*. Direct comparisons are formed with di, e.g. più caro di ... [pyoo **ka**ro dee] *(more expensive than ...).*

Some adjectives do not follow this pattern, e.g. buono – migliore – ottimo [**bwo**no – meel**yo**ray – o**tte**emo] *(good – better – best)*; cattivo – peggiore – pessimo [ka**tte**evo – pe**jo**ray – **pess**eemo] *(bad – worse – worst).*

Another form of the superlative, the absolute superlative, can be created with the ending -**issimo**: bellissimo [belle**esse**emo] *(very beautiful)*; carissimo [kare**esse**emo] *(very expensive).*

Adverbs

The adverb is usually derived from the feminine form of the adjective by the addition of the suffix -**mente**: chiaro/chiara [**kya**ro/**kya**ra] – chiaramente [kyara**men**tay] *(clearly, obviously)*; Chiaramente vengo domani da te. [kyara**men**tay **ven**go do**ma**nee da tay] *(I will obviously come to see you tomorrow.)*

Irregular adverbs are: bene [**bay**nay] *(well)*, male [**ma**lay] *(badly)*: Tutto bene. [**too**tto **bay**nay] *(Everything is fine.)*; Dove fa male? [**do**vay fa **ma**lay] *(Where does it hurt?)*

Pronouns

Subject pronouns

io [**ee**-o] *(I)*
tu [too] *(you [singular/familiar])*
lui [**loo**-ee] *(he)*; lei [lay] *(she)*; lei [lay] *(you [singular/formal])*
noi [noy] *(we)*
voi [voy] *(you [plural/familiar])*
loro [**lo**ro] *(they)*; Loro [**lo**ro] *(you [plural/formal]).*

Object pronouns

mi [mee] *(me/to me)*
ti [tee] *(you/to you [singular/familiar])*
gli [lyee] *(to him)*; le [lay] *(to her)*; Le [lay] *(to you [singular/formal])*
lo [lo] *(him)*; la [la] *(her)*; La [la] *] (you [singular/formal])*
ci [chee] *(us)*
vi [vee] *(you [plural/familiar])*
gli [lyee] *(to them)*; Loro [**lo**ro] *(to you [plural/formal])*
li [lee] *(them [m])*; le [lay] *(them [f])*; Li [lee] *(you [m])*; Le [lay] *(you [f] [plural/formal])*

Possessive pronouns

mio/mia [**mee**-o/**mee**-a] *(my)*
tuo/tua [**too**-o/**too**-a] *(your [singular/familiar])*
suo/sua [**soo**-o/**soo**-a] *(his; her; your [singular/formal])*
nostro/nostra [**nos**tro/**nos**tra] *(our)*
vostro/vostra [**vos**tro/**vos**tra] *(your [plural/familiar])*
loro [**lo**ro] *(their)*;
Loro [**lo**ro] *(your [plural/formal]).*

The possessive pronouns are used with both the definite and indefinite articles, e.g. la mia casa [la **mee**-a **ka**za] *(my house)*; una mia amica [**oo**na **mee**-a a**mee**ka] *(one of my friends).*

Other uses include a casa mia [a **ka**za **mee**-a] *(at my house; to my house)*; a casa nostra [a **ka**za **nos**tra] *(at our house; to our house).*

Demonstrative pronouns

questo [**kwes**to] *(this [m. sing])* –
questi [**kwes**tee] *(these [m.plural])*;
questa [**kwes**ta] *(this [f.sing])* – queste
[**kwes**tay] *(these [f.plural])* - quello
[**kwel**lo] *(that [m.sing])* – quelli
[**kwel**lee] *(those [m.plural])* - quella
[**kwel**la] *(that [f.sing])* – quelle
[**kwel**lay] *(those [f.plural])*

Questo and quello can be used without
a noun, e.g. Cosa è questo? [**ko**za ay
kwesto] *(What is this?)*.

Prepositions

di [dee] *(from, of)*
a [a] *(to, at)*
da [da] *(from, of, to)*
in [een] *(in, to)*
con [kon] *(with, through)*
su [soo] *(on, above)*

The prepositions **di**, **a**, **da**, **in** and **su**
merge with the definite article:
di+il = del [del]
di+lo = dello [**del**lo]
di+la = della [**del**la]
di+i = dei [**day**ee]
di+gli = degli [**day**lyee]
di+le = delle [**del**lay]

There are also the forms al (a+il) [al], allo
(a+lo) [**al**lo], ai (a+i) [a-ee], dal (da+il)
[dal], nel (in+il) [nel] and sul (su+il) [sool],
e.g. Penso alle ferie. [**pen**so **al**lay **fair**yay]
(I am thinking of the holidays.); sul
tavolo [sool **ta**volo] *(on the table)*.

Verbs

There are three groups of regular verbs.
Their endings are -**are**, -**ere** and -**ire**.
Pronouns are usually left out, as the verb
subject is usually indicated by the ending.

Present tense of regular verbs

-**are**: mandare [man**da**ray] *(to send)*
io mando [**ee**-o **man**do] *(I send)*
tu mandi [too **man**dee] *(you
[singular/familiar] send)*
lui/lei/Lei manda[loo-ee/**lay man**da]
(he/she sends; you [sing./formal] send)

noi mandiamo [noy man**dya**mo] *(we send)*
voi mandate [voy man**da**tay] *(you
[plural/familiar] send)*
loro/Loro mandano [**loro man**dano]
(they send; you [plural/formal] send)

-**ere**: vendere [**ven**deray] *(to sell)*
io vendo [**ee**-o **ven**do] *(I sell)*
tu vendi [too **ven**dee] *(you
[singular/familiar] send)*
lui/lei/Lei venda[loo-ee/**lay ven**da]
(he/she sells; you [sing./formal] sell)
noi vendiamo [noy ven**dya**mo] *(we send)*
voi vendete [voy ven**det**tay] *(you
[plural/familiar] sell)*
loro/Loro vendono [**loro ven**dono] *(they
sell; you [plural/formal] sell)*

-**ire**: partire [par**ti**ray] *(to leave)*
io parto [**ee**-o **par**to] *(I leave)*
tu parti [too **par**tee] *(you
[singular/familiar] leave)*
lui/lei/Lei parte [loo-ee/**lay par**tay] *(he/
she leaves; you [singular/formal] leave)*
noi partiamo [noy par**tya**mo] *(we leave)*
voi partite [voy par**tee**tay] *(you
[plural/familiar] leave)*
loro/Loro partono [**loro par**tono] *(they
leave; you [plural/formal] leave)*

Present tense of some irregular verbs

avere [a**vai**ray] *(to have)*
io ho [**ee**-oo] *(I have)*
tu hai [too a-ee] *(you [singular/
familiar] have)*
lui/lei/Lei ha [loo-ee/**lay** a] *(he/she
has); you [singular/formal] have)*
noi abbiamo [noy ab**bya**mo] *(we have)*
voi avete [voy a**vay**tay] *(you
[plural/familiar] have)*
loro/Loro hanno [**loro an**no] *(they
have; you [plural/formal] have)*

essere [**ess**airay] *(to be)*
io sono [**ee**-o **so**no] *(I am)*
tu sei [too **say**] *(you [singular/
familiar] are)*
lui/lei/Lei è [loo-ee/**lay** ay] *(he/she is;
you [singular/formal] are)*
noi siamo [**noy sya**mo] *(we are)*
voi siete [voy s**yay**tay] *(you [plural/
familiar] are)*
loro/Loro sono [**loro so**no] *(they are;
you [plural/ formal] are)*

andare [andaray] *(to go)*
io vado [**ee**-o **va**do] *(I go)*
tu vai [too **va**-ee] *(you [singular/familiar] go)*
lui/lei/Lei va [**loo**-ee/**lay** va] *(he/she goes; you [singular/formal] go)*
noi andiamo [noy and**ya**mo] *(we go)*
voi andate [voy an**da**tay] *(you [plural/familiar] go)*
loro/Loro vanno [**loro vanno**] *(they go; you [plural/ formal] go)*

fare [**fa**ray] *(to make, to do)*
io faccio [**ee**-o **fa**cho] *(I do)*
tu fai [too **fa**-ee] *(you [singular/familiar] do)*
lui/lei/Lei fa [**loo**-ee/**lay** fa] *(he/she does; you [singular/formal] do)*
noi facciamo [noy fa**cha**mo] *(we do)*
voi fate [voy **fa**tay] *(you [plural/familiar] do)*
loro/Loro fanno [**loro fan**no] *(they do; you [plural/formal] do)*

potere [po**tai**ray] *(to be able to)*
io posso [**ee**-o **pos**so] *(I can)*
tu puoi [too pwoy] *(you [singular/familiar] can)*
lui/lei/Lei può [**loo**-ee/**lay** pwo] *(he/she can; you [singular/ formal] can)*
noi possiamo [noy pos**sya**mo] *(we can)*
voi potete [voy po**tay**tay] *(you [plural/familiar] can)*
loro/Loro possono [**loro pos**sono] *(they can; you [plural/formal] can)*

venire [ve**nee**ray] *(to come)*
io vengo [**ee**-o **ven**go] *(I come)*
tu vieni [too **vyay**nee] *(you [singular/familiar] come)*
lui/lei/Lei viene [**loo**-ee/**lay vyay**nay] *(he/she comes; you [singular/ formal] come)*
noi veniamo [noy ven**ya**mo] *(we come)*
voi venite [voy ve**nee**tay] *(you [plural/familiar] come)*
loro/Loro vengono [**loro ven**gono] *(they come; you [plural/formal] come)*

volere [vo**lai**ray] *(to wish/to want)*
io voglio [**ee**-o **vol**yo] *(I wish/want)*
tu vuoi [too vwoy] *(you [singular/familiar] wish/want)*
lui/lei/Lei vuole [**loo**-ee/**lay vwo**lay] *(he/she wishes/wants; you [singular/formal] wish/want)*
noi vogliamo [noy vol**ya**mo] *(we wish/want)*
voi volete [voy vo**lay**tay] *(you [plural/familiar] wish/want)*
loro/Loro vogliono [**loro vol**yono] *(they wish/want; you [plural/formal] wish)*

Perfect

The perfect tense in Italian is formed with the auxiliary verb **avere** *(to have)* or **essere** *(to be)* and the past participle:

io ho avuto [**ee**o-o a**voo**to] *(I have had)*
tu hai avuto [too a-ee a**voo**to] *(you have had)*
lui/lei ha avuto [**loo**-ee/**lay** a a**voo**to] *(he/she has had)*
noi abbiamo avuto [noy ab**bya**mo a**voo**to] *(we have had)*
voi avete avuto [voy a**vay**tay a**voo**to] *(you [plural/familiar] have had)*
loro hanno avuto [**loro an**no a**voo**to] *(they have had)*

io sono stato *(m)*/stata *(f)* [**ee**-o **so**no **sta**to/**sta**ta] *(I have been)*
tu sei stato *(m)*/stata *(f)* [too say **sta**to/**sta**ta] *(you [singular/familiar] have been)*
lui/lei è stato *(m)*/stata *(f)* [**loo**-ee/lay ay **sta**to/**sta**ta] *(he/she has been)*
noi siamo stati *(m)*/state *(f)* [noy **sya**mo **sta**tee/**sta**tay] *(we have been)*
voi siete stati *(m)*/state *(f)* [voy **syay**tay **sta**tee/**sta**tay] *(you [plural/familiar] have been)*
loro sono stati *(m)*/state *(f)* [**loro so**no **sta**tee/**sta**tay] *(they have been)*

Negatives

The negative **non** always precedes the verb, e.g. Non parlo italiano. [non **par**lo eetal**ya**no] *(I don't speak Italian.)*
Niente *(nothing)* and **mai** *(never)* require a double negative, e.g. Non ho niente. [non o n**yen**tay] *(I have nothing)*

Two people-watchers on the piazza

General

Hello and goodbye

Good morning/afternoon.	Buon giorno. [bwon **jor**no]
Good evening.	Buona sera. [bw**o**na **sair**a]
Good night.	Buona notte. [bw**o**na **not**tay]
Hello!	Ciao! [chow]
How are you doing?	Come va? [**ko**may va]
How are you?	Come stai?/Come sta?
	[**ko**may sta-ee/**ko**may sta]

* Bene, grazie. [**bay**nay **grat**syay] Fine, thank you.

And you?	E tu?/E Lei? [ay too/ay lay/]
Goodbye.	Arrivederci. [arreevay**dair**chee]
Bye.	Ciao! [chow]
See you soon.	A fra poco. [a fra **pok**ko]
See you tomorrow.	A domani. [a do**man**ee]
Regards to the family.	Saluti alla famiglia. [sa**loo**tee **a**lla fa**meel**ya]
Thank you for everything.	Grazie di tutto. [**grat**syay dee **too**to]
We really enjoyed it.	Ci è piaciuto molto. [chee ay pee-a**choo**to **mol**to]

* Buon viaggio! [bwon **vyaj**jo] Have a good journey!

Introducing yourself

Mr/Mrs/Miss ...	Signore/Signora/Signorina ...
	[seen**yo**ray/seen**yo**ra/seenyo**ree**na]
What's your name?	Come ti chiami?/Come si chiama?
	[**ko**may tee **kyam**ee/**ko**may see **kyam**a]
My name is ...	Mi chiamo ... [mee **kyam**o]

12

This is/These are	Questo è/Questa è/Questi sono
	[**kwes**to ay/**kwes**ta ay/**kwes**tee **so**no]
my husband/my boyfriend	mio marito/il mio amico
	[**mee**-o mareeto/eel **mee**-o ameeko]
my wife/my girlfriend	mia moglie/la mia amica
	[**mee**-a **mol**yay/la **mee**-a ameeka]
my son/my daughter/	mio figlio/mia figlia/i miei figli. [**mee**-o
my children.	**feel**yo/**mee**-a **feel**ya/ee myayee feelyee]
Pleased to meet you.	Piacere./Molto lieto. [peea**chai**ray/**mol**to **lyay**to]
And you.	Altrettanto. [altray**tan**to]
Where are you from?	Di dove sei?/Di dov'è? [dee **do**vay say/dee dovay]

I'm	Io sono [ee-o sono]
English	inglese [een**glay**zay]
American	americano/-a [amereekano/-a]
Australian	australiano/-a. [owstralyano/-a]
We live in .../	Noi abitiamo a .../in hotel ...
stay at the ... Hotel	[**no**-ee abee**tya**mo a/een o**tel**]

Communication

Do you speak English?	Tu parli/Lei parla/ inglese?
	[too **par**lee/lay **par**la een**glay**zay]
What's that called?	Come si chiama questo? [**ko**may see kyama **kwes**to]
Pardon?/Sorry??	Come prego? [**ko**may **pray**go]
What does that mean?	Cosa significa questo? [**ko**za seenyee**fee**ka **kwes**to]
Did you understand that?	Hai/Ha capito? [a-ee/a ka**pee**to]
I don't understand.	Io non capisco. [**ee**-o non ka**pee**sko]
Could you speak more slowly, please?	Prego lentamente! [**pray**go lenta**men**tay]
Could you repeat that, please?	Prego un'altra volta! [**pray**go oon**al**tra **vol**ta]

Could you ... for me?	Può/Puoi [pwo/pwoy]
write that down	scrivermelo [**skree**vairmaylo]
explain/translate that	chiarire/tradurre? [keea**ree**ray/tra**doo**ray]

Civilities

Please.	Prego. [**pray**go]
Thank you (very much).	(Molte) grazie. [(**mol**tay) **grats**yay]
Thank you, the same to you.	Grazie, altrettanto. [**grats**yay altre**tan**to]
Thank you for your help.	Grazie per l'aiuto. [**grats**yay pair la**yoo**to]
* Prego./Non c'è di che. [**pray**go/non chay dee kay]	You're welcome./Don't mention it.
Sorry/Excuse me.	Scusa/Scusi.
	[**skoo**za/**skoo**zee]
* Non fa niente. [non fa **nyen**tay]	It doesn't matter.

13

Do you have a moment, please! Un momento, prego! [oon momento praygo]

That's very nice of you. É molto gentile da parte tua/sua.
[ay molto jenteelay da partay too-a/soo-a]

I'm sorry about that. Mi dispiace. [mee deespyachay]
That's a pity. Peccato. [pekato]

Welcome! Un cordiale benvenuto! [oon kordyalay benvenooto]
Congratulations! Cordiali auguri! [kordyalee owgooree]
Happy birthday! Auguri (per il compleanno)!
[owgooree (pair eel komplayanno)]

Have fun! Buon divertimento! [bwon deevairteemento]
Get well soon! Buona guarigione! [bwona gwareejonay]
Good luck! Molto successo! [molto soochaysso]

Have a nice day! Una bella giornata! [oona bella jornata]
Have a good journey! Buon viaggio! [bwon vyajjo]
Have a good holiday! Buone vacanze! [bwonay vakantsay]
Merry Christmas! Buon Natale! [bwon natalay]
Happy New Year! Felice Anno nuovo! [feleechay anno nwovo]

Meeting people

Do you mind if I sit here? Posso sedermi con te/con Lei?
[posso sedairmee kon tay/kon lay]

Do you mind? Permetti? [pairmettee]

Are you **Sei/È** [say/ay]
  on you own   solo (-a) in giro [solo (-a) een jeero]
  travelling with somebody   con qualcuno in giro [kon kwalkoono een jeero]
  married?   sposato (-a)? [spozato (-a)]

Do you have a Hai un amico/un'amica?
boyfriend/girlfriend? [a-ee oon ameeko/oon ameeka]

How old are you? Quanti anni hai? [kwantee annee a-ee]
I am 25 years old. Io ho venticinque anni.
[ee-o o venteecheenkway annee]

What do you do for a living? Che lavoro fai/fa? [kay lavoro fa-ee/fa]

I'm **Sono** [sono]
  still at school   scolaro (scolara) [skolaro (skolara)]
  a student   studente (studentessa)
  [stoodayntay (stoodayntessa)]
  employed.   impiegata (impiegato). [eempeeaygata/(-o)]

Can I buy you a drink? Vuoi/Vuole bere qualcosa? [vwoy/ vwolay bairay kwalkoza]

Thank you, that's a nice idea. Si, volentieri, buona idea.
[see volentyairee bwona eedaya]

Why not? Perché no? [pairkay no]
No, thank you. No grazie. [no gratsyay]
Perhaps another time. Forse un'altra volta. [forsay oonaltra volta]
Maybe later. Forse più tardi. [forsay pyoo tardee]

Do you like it here? Ti/Le piace qui. [tee/lay pyachay kwee]

Greetings

Buon giorno means "good morning" and also "hello" or "good-day". In the early evening, the normal greeting is *buona sera*. *Buona notte* is used later in the evening to bid someone goodnight. A more easy-going greeting, however, is *ciao (hello/goodbye)*. The formal way to say goodbye is *arrivederci/ arrivederla! (until the next time!)*. *Come stai/sta? (how are you?)* is often added to the initial greeting, but nobody expects an honest answer to the question. It is best to respond with a simple *bene (OK)* or *molto bene (very well)*.

I like it very much here.	Mi piace molto. [mee **pya**chay **mol**to]
Is this your first time here?	Sei/È qui per la prima volta? [say/ay kwee pair la **pree**ma **vol**ta]
No, I've been to … before.	No, sono già stato (-a) una volta a … [no **so**no ja **sta**to (-a) **oo**na **vol**ta a]
Have you ever been to England? You must visit me.	Conosci/Conosce la Inghilterra? [ko**no**shee/ko**no**shay la eengeel**tai**ra] Vienimi a trovare./Mi venga a trovare. [vye**nee**mee a tro**va**ray/mee **ven**ga a tro**va**ray]
Here's my address.	Questo è il mio indirizzo. [**kwes**to ay eel **mee**-o eendee**ree**tzo]
How long have you been staying here? For a week./For two days.	Da quanto tempo sei/è già qui? [da **kwan**to **tem**po say/ay ja kwee] Da una settimana/due giorni. [da **oo**na setee**ma**na/**doo**ay **jor**nee]
How much longer are you staying? Another week/two days.	Quanto tempo rimani/rimane ancora qui? [**kwan**to **tem**po ree**ma**nee/ree**ma**nay an**ko**ra kwee] Ancora una settimana/due giorni. [an**ko**ra **oo**na setee**ma**na/**doo**ay **jor**nee]

Shall we … together today/tomorrow?	**Vogliamo oggi/domani … insieme?** [vol**ya**mo **oj**jee/do**ma**nee … een**sya**ymay]
have a meal	mangiare [man**ja**ray]
go out	uscire [oo**shee**ray]
go to the cinema/go dancing	andare al cinema/a ballare [an**da**ray al **chee**nayma/a bal**la**ray]
do something sporty	fare dello sport [**fa**ray **del**lo sport]
play	giocare [jo**ka**ray]
O.K., let's do that!	D'accordo, va bene! [da**kor**do va **bay**nay]
No, thank you.	No, grazie. [no **grats**yay]
I can't, sorry.	Mi dispiace non posso. [mee deesp**ya**chay non **pos**so]
What time/Where shall we meet?	Quando/Dove ci incontriamo? [**kwan**do/**do**vay chee eenkontr**ya**mo]
At 7 o'clock in front of the cinema.	Alle sette davanti al cinema. [**al**-lay **set**tay da**van**tee al **chee**nayma]

Shall I
  pick you up
  take you home

  take you to the bus stop?

No, that's not necessary.

It's been very nice.

When can we see each other again?
I don't like that.

I don't feel like it.

Leave me alone!

Please go away!

Posso venire a [posso veneeray a]
  prenderti/prenderla [**pren**dairtee/**pren**dairla]
  accompagnarti/accompagnarla a casa
  [akompany**ar**tee/akompany**ar**la a **ka**za]
  accompagnarti/accompagnarla all'autobus?
  [akompany**ar**tee/akompany**ar**la al-**ow**toboos]

No, grazie non è necessario.
[no **grats**yay non ay neche**ssar**yo]
È stato molto bello. [ay **sta**to **mol**to **bel**lo]

Quando ci incontriamo di nuovo?
[**kwan**do chee eenkontr**yam**o dee nwovo]
Questo non mi piace.
[**kwes**to non mee py**a**chay]
Non ne ho voglia. [non nay o **vol**ya]

Lasciami/Mi lasci/ in pace!
[**la**shamee/mee **la**shee een **pa**chay]
Per favore, vattene/se ne vada/.
[pair fa**vor**ay **va**tenay/say nay **va**da]

Questions

What's that?
How much is that?
Where is ...?/can I get ...?
Where does ... go?
How do you say it?
What's that called?
How long does it last?
When does the concert start?

How many kilometres/minutes is it?

Cosa è questo? [**ko**za ay **kwes**to]
Quanto costa questo? [**kwan**to **kos**ta **kwes**to]
Dov'è ...?/C'è ...? [do**vay**/chay]
Dove va ...? [**do**vay va]
Come si dice? [**ko**may see **dee**chay]
Come si chiama [**ko**may see ky**a**ma]
Quanto dura? [**kwan**to **doo**ra]
Quando comincia il concerto?
[**kwan**do ko**meen**cha eel kon**chair**to]
Quanti chilometri/minuti sono?
[**kwan**tee keelo**me**tree/mee**noo**tee **so**no]

Could you
  help me
  show me, please?

Can I help you?

Puoi/Può [pwoi/pwo]
  aiutarmi [ayoo**tar**mee]
  mostrarmi questo? [mos**trar**mee **kwes**to]

Posso aiutarti/aiutarla? [**pos**so ayoo**tar**tee/la]

Interrogatives

What?
Who?
Which?
Where?/Where to?
How?
How much
How many?
When?
How long?
Why?
What ... for?

Cosa? [**ko**za]
Chi? [kee]
Quale? *(Sing)* [**kwa**lay]; Quali? *(Pl)* [**kwa**lee]
Dove? [**do**vay]
Come? [**ko**may]
Quanto [**kwan**to]
Quanti *(m/Pl)* [**kwan**tee]/Quante *(f/Pl)* [**kwan**tay]
Quando? [**kwan**do]
Per quanto tempo? [pair **kwan**to **tem**po]
Perché? [pair**kay**]
Per cosa? [pair **ko**za]

Days of the week

Monday lunedì [loonaydee]
Tuesday martedì [martaydee]
Wednesday mercoledì [mairkolaydee]
Thursday giovedì [jovaydee]
Friday venerdì [venairdee]
Saturday sabato [sabato]
Sunday domenica [domeneeka]

Months

January gennaio [jennayo]
February febbraio [febbrayo]
March marzo [martso]
April aprile [apreelay]
May maggio [majjo]

June giugno [joonyo]
July luglio [loolyo]
August agosto [agosto]
September settembre [settembray]
October ottobre [ottobray]
November novembre [novembray]
December dicembre [deechembray]

Seasons

spring primavera [preemavaira]
summer estate [estatay]
autumn autunno [owtoonno]
winter inverno [eenvairno]
peak/off peak season alta/fuori
    stagione [alta/fworee stajonay]

Time

What's the (exact) time, please?

Che ore sono (di preciso), prego?
[kay oray sono (dee precheezo) praygo]

It's
  1 o'clock/2 o'clock
  quarter past three
  quarter to five

  twenty past three
  half past three
  five to six
  noon/midnight.

È/Sono [ay/sono]
  l'una/le due [loona/lay dooay]
  le tre e un quarto [lay tray ay oon kwarto]
  le cinque meno un quarto
  [lay cheenkway mayno oon kwarto]
  le quindici e venti [lay kweendeechee ay ventee]
  le tre e mezza [lay tray ay metza]
  le sei meno cinque [lay say mayno cheenkway]
  mezzogiorno/mezzanotte.
  [metzojorno/metzanottay]

What time do we have to be there?
Around twelve/At twelve o'clock sharp.
When is breakfast/ lunch/dinner?

A che ora dobbiamo essere lì?
[a kay ora dobbyamo essairay lee]
Più o meno alle dodici/Alle dodici in punto.
[pyoo o mayno allay dodeechee/... een poonto]
Quando c'è colazione/pranzo/cena?
[kwando chay kolatsyonay/prandzo/chayna]

* Dalle otto alle nove.
[dallay otto allay novay]

From eight to nine.

Date

What's the date today?

Che giorno è oggi?
[kay jorno ay ojjee]

Today's the 1st/2nd/15th of August.

Oggi è il primo/due/quindici agosto.
[ojjee ay eel preemo/dooay/kweendeechee agosto]

We'll arrive on the 20th of May.

Noi arriviamo il venti maggio.
[noy areevyamo eel ventee majjo]

17

| We're staying until August 31st. | Noi rimaniamo fino al trentuno agosto. [noy reemanyamo **fee**no al trentoo**no** a**gos**to] |
| I was born on January 12th (1960). | Sono nato il dodici gennaio (millenovecentosessanta). [sono **na**to eel **do**deechee jen**na**yo (meelaynovaychentosessanta)] |

Indication of time

in the evening	la sera [la **sai**ra]
at the weekend	a fine settimana [a **fee**nay sette**e**mana]
until tomorrow	fino a domani [**fee**no a do**ma**nee]
yesterday	ieri [ee**ai**ree]
today	oggi [**oj**jee]
tonight	stasera [sta**sai**ra]
in a fortnight	fra quindici giorni [fra **kween**deechee **jor**nee]
(this/next/every) year	(quest'/il prossimo/passato/ogni) anno [(**kwest**/eel **pros**seemo/**on**yee) **an**no]
last year	l'anno scorso [**lan**no **skor**so]
now	adesso [a**des**so]
sometimes	qualche volta [**kwal**kay **vol**ta]
minute	minuto [mee**noo**to]
at midday	a mezzogiorno [a metzo**jor**no]
tomorrow	domani [do**ma**nee]
in the morning	la mattina [la mat**tee**na]
in the afternoon	il pomeriggio [eel pomai**ree**jo]
at night	la notte [la **not**tay]
in time	per tempo [pair **tem**po]
second	secondo [se**kon**do]
late/too late	tardi/troppo tardi [**tar**dee/**trop**po **tar**dee]
later	più tardi [pyoo **tar**dee]
hour	l'ora [**lo**ra]
daily	giornalmente [jornal**men**tay]
day	giorno [**jor**no]
day after tomorrow	dopodomani [doppodo**ma**nee]
(two days) ago	(due giorni) fa [(**doo**ay **jor**nee) fa]
day before yesterday	l'altro ieri [**lal**tro ee**ai**ree]
before	prima [**pree**ma]
week	settimana [sette**e**mana]
at the moment	al momento [al mo**men**to]

Measurements

centimetre/metre/kilometre	centimetro/metro/chilometro [chen**tee**metro/**me**tro/kee**lo**metro]
square metre/square kilometre/hectare	metro quadrato/chilometro quadrato/ettaro [**me**tro kwa**dra**to/kee**lo**metro kwa**dra**to/**et**taro]
cubic metre	metro cubo [**me**tro **koo**bo]
kilometres per hour	chilometri orari [kee**lo**metree o**ra**ree]
quarter of a litre	un quarto di litro [oon **kwar**to dee **lee**tro]
half a litre	mezzo litro [**met**zo **lee**tro]
gram/half a kilo/ kilogramme/ton	grammo/mezzo chilo/chilo/tonnellata [**gram**mo/**met**zo **kee**lo/**kee**lo/tonnay**la**ta]
second/minute/hour	secondo/minuto/ora [se**kon**do/mee**noo**to/**o**ra]

day/week/month/year	giorno/settimana/mese/anno [jorno/setteemana/mayzay/anno]
a dozen/a couple/a portion	una dozzina/un paio/una porzione [oona dotzeena/oon pa-yo/oona portsyonay]

Weather

Is it going to stay nice/bad	Rimane così bello/brutto? [reemanay kozee bello/brootto]
What does the weather forecast say?	Cosa dice la previsione del tempo? [koza deechay la preveezyonay del tempo]
It's going to get colder/warmer.	Farà freddo/caldo. [fara frayddo/kaldo]
It is hot/close/ stormy/foggy.	È caldo/afoso/tempestoso/nebbioso. [ay kaldo/afozo/tempestozo/nebyozo]
It is windy.	C'è vento. [chay vento]
It is going to rain/snow today/tomorrow.	Oggi/Domani dovrebbe piovere/nevicare. [ojjee/ domanee dovrebbay pyovairay/neveekaray]
For how long has it been raining?	Da quanto tempo piove già? [da kwanto tempo pyovay ja]
When is it going to stop raining?	Quando smette di piovere? [kwando zmettay dee pyovairay]
What's the temperature?	Quanti gradi abbiamo? [kwantee gradee abbyamo]
25 degrees (in the shade).	Venticinque gradi. [venteecheenkway gradee]

Colours

I'm looking for a pair of blue/black trousers.	Io cerco pantaloni blu/neri. [ee-o chairko pantalonee bloo/nairee]
Do you have this shirt	**Ha questa camicia** [a kwesta kameecha]
in white, too	anche in bianco [ankay een byanko]
in another colour?	in un altro colore? [een oon altro koloray]
I don't like this colour.	Questo colore non mi piace. [kwesto koloray non mee pyachay]
This colour is too light/dark	Questo colore è troppo chiaro/troppo scuro. [kwesto koloray ay troppo kyaro/troppo skooro]

Colours and patterns

beige beige [bayj]
black nero/-a [nairo/-a]
blue blu [bloo]
brown marrone [marronay]
checked a quadri [a kwadree]
colourful colorato/-a [kolorato/-a]
dark scuro/-a [skooro/-a]
green verde [vairday]
grey grigio/-a [greejo/-a]
light chiaro/-a [kyaro/-a]

patterned stampato/-a [stampato/-a]
pink rosa [roza]
plain-coloured tinta unita [teenta ooneeta]
purple viola [vyola]
red rosso/-a [rosso/-a]
striped rigato/-a [reegato/-a]
turquoise turchese [toorkayzay]
white bianco/-a [byanko/-a]
yellow giallo/-a [jallo/-a]

It's often a tight squeeze for traffic in the medieval town centres

Getting Around

Customs formalities

* Il Suo passaporto, prego!
[eel soo-o passaporto praygo]

Your passport, please!

* La Sua patente, prego!
[la soo-a patentay praygo]

Your driving licence, please!

* I documenti della macchina, prego! [ee dokoomentee della makkena praygo]

Your vehicle registration papers, please!

* Lei dove è diretto?
[lay dovay ay deeraytto]

Where are you going to?

I'm/We're going to ...

Io vado/Noi andiamo a ...
[ee-o vado/noy andyamo a]

I'm
  a tourist.
  on a business trip.

Io sono [eeo sono]
  turista [tooreesta]
  in viaggio di affari. [een vyajjo dee affaree]

How many ... are duty free?

Quanti *(m)*/**Quante** *(f)* **... sono liberi da dogana?**
[kwantee/kwantay ... sono leebairee da dogana]

  cigarettes
  litres of wine/spirit

  sigarette [seegarayttay]
  litri di vino/liquore [leetree dee veeno/leekworay]

*Prego apra il cofano!
[praygo apra eel kofano]

Open the suitcase, please!

Can I call
  my embassy
  my consulate

Posso parlare con [posso parlaray kon]
  la mia ambasciata [la mee-a ambashata]
  il mio consolato? [eel mee-o konsolato]

Asking Directions

How do I get
to ...
on to the motorway
to the city centre
to ... Square
to ... Street
to the station/bus station

to the airport/harbour?

Come arrivo [komay arreevo]
a ... [a]
all'autostrada [alla-ootostrada]
al centro [al chentro]
in piazza ... [een pyatza]
in via ... [een veea]
alla stazione/alla stazione dei pullman
[alla statssyonay/alla stasyonay dayee poolman]
all'aeroporto/al porto? [al-airoporto/al porto]

* All'incrocio [alleenkrocho]   At the crossroads
* Dopo il semaforo   After the traffic lights
[dopo eel semaforo]

* **Dopo cinquecento metri**   **After 500 metres**
[dopo cheenkwaychento maytree]
  * girare a destra/sinistra   turn right/left
[jeeraray a destra/seeneestra]
  * andare dritto   go straight ahead
[andaray dreetto]
  * tornare indietro.   turn around.
[tornaray eendyaytro]

Is this the road to ...?   È questa la strada per ...?
                       [ay kwesta la strada pair]

How far is it to...?   Quanto è lontano fino a ...?
                       [kwanto ay lontano feeno a]

Can you show me that on the   Può indicarmelo sulla carta?
map?   [pwo eendeekarmaylo soolla karta]

Car, motorbike and bicycle hire

I'd like to hire
a car
a four-wheel drive
a minibus
a camper van
a motorbike
a moped
a scooter
a bicycle
a mountain bike
for two days/one week

from today/tomorrow

Io vorrei affittare [eeo vorrayee affeettaray]
una macchina [oona makkeena]
un fuoristrada [oon fworeestrada]
un pullmino [oon poolmeeno]
un camper [oon kampair]
una motocicletta [oona motocheekletta]
un motorino [oon motoreeno]
una vespa [oona vespa]
una bicicletta [oona beecheekletta]
una mountainbike [oona maoontenbaeek]
per due giorni/una settimana
[pair dooay jornee/oona setteemana]
da oggi/domani. [da ojjee/domanee]

What do you charge

per day/per week

per kilometre?

Quanto costa questo veicolo
[kwanto kosta kwesto vayeekolo]
al giorno/alla settimana
[al jorno/alla setteemana]
secondo i chilometri percorsi?
[sekondo ee keelometree pairkorsee]

Is there a mileage limit?	C'è un limite di chilometraggio? [chay un **lee**meetay dee keelome**traj**jo]
Is there a free allowance?	È senza limite di chilometraggio? [ay **sen**tsa **lee**meetay dee keelome**traj**jo]
How many kilometres are included in the price?	Quanti kilometri sono liberi? [**kwan**tee keelo**me**tree **so**no **lee**bairee]
What petrol does it take?	Quale benzina devo mettere? [**kwa**lay ben**dzee**na **day**vo **met**tairay]
How much is the deposit?	Quant'è la cauzione? [**kwan**tay la ka-oots**yo**nay]
Does the vehicle have comprehensive insurance?	Questo veicolo ha una polizza di assicurazione kasko? [**kwes**to vay**ee**kolo a **oo**na po**lee**tza dee asseekoorats**yo**nay **kas**ko]
Can I take the car back in … hours/days?	Posso portare questo veicolo in … ore/giorni indietro? [**pos**so por**ta**ray **kwes**to vay**ee**kolo een … **o**ray/**jor**nee een**dyay**tro]
When do I have to be back by?	Fino a quando devo portare questo veicolo indietro? [**fee**no a **kwan**do **day**vo por**ta**ray **kwes**to vay**ee**kolo een**dyay**tro]
Could you explain how everything works, please!	Per favore mi spieghi precisamente tutte le funzioni. [pair fa**vo**ray mee **spyay**gee precheeza**men**tay **toot**tay lay foonts**yo**nee]

Parking

Can I park here?	Posso parcheggiare qui? [**pos**so parkay**ja**ray kwee]
Is there a … near here?	**C'è … qui vicino** [chay … kwee vee**chee**no]
a (supervised) car park	un parcheggio (custodito) [oon par**kay**jo (koosto**dee**to)]
a (multi-storey) car park/ a garage	un autosilo/un garage? [oon owto**see**lo/oon ga**ra**jay]

Traffic signs

Accendere i fari Use your headlights!
Attenzione Caution!
Autostrada (con obbligo di pedaggio) motorway (subject to toll)
Camion lorries
Cantiere edile construction site
Cassa toll booth
Circonvallazione bypass
Coda traffic jam
Controllo radar radar control
Corsia slow lane
Corsia per ciclisti cycle track

Curva pericolosa dangerous bend
Dare la precedenza give way
Deviazione diversion
Disco orario parking disc
Divieto di parcheggio no parking
Divieto di sorpasso no overtaking
Autosilo car park
Guidare a destra keep right
Lasciare libera l'uscita keep clear
Lavori in corso road works
Pericolo danger
Rallentare reduce speed
Senso unico one-way-street
Vicolo cieco cul de sac

Travelling by car

The Italians are very attached to their cars and drive everywhere. In Italy about 75 percent of all journeys are made by car and so the Italian road network is very extensive. Motorways *(autostrade)* criss-cross the whole country. All of them levy a toll except the section from Salerno to Reggio Calabria.

The customer is still king at the petrol station *(distributore)*. Attended service is the norm rather than the exception. If requested, the pump attendant will clean your windscreen and check your oil and water. He will take your money and will expect a small tip. Only at night or on Sunday is a self-service system in operation and for this you will need a good supply of high-value notes.

You will find plenty of small garages *(officina)* in every town. To call the Italian Automobile Club *(ACI)*, if you have a breakdown, dial 116. The emergency number *(Numero di Emergenza)* is 113.

Is the car park open during the night?

È aperto di notte il parcheggio? [ay apairto dee nottay eel parkayjo]

* Occupato. [okkoopato]
* Libero. [leebairo]

Full.
Spaces.

How much is it

per hour
per day
per night?

Quanto è la tariffa di parcheggio [kwanto ay la tareeffa dee parkayjo]
all'ora [allora]
al giorno [al jorno]
a notte? [a nottay]

Petrol

Where's the nearest petrol station, please?

Dov'è il prossimo distributore di benzina? [dovay eel prosseemo deestreebootoray dee bendzeena]

Fill up, please.

Prego il pieno. [praygo eel pyayno]

20 litres of . . . , please.
regular
super
diesel
unleaded/leaded.

mixture for a two-stroke engine.

Prego venti litri di [praygo ventee leetree dee]
benzina normale [bendzeena normalay]
benzina super [bendzeena soopair]
diesel [deezel]
senza piombo/con piombo [sendsa pyombo/kon pyombo]
miscela a due tempi. [meeshayla a dooay tempee]

I'd like half a litre of oil, please.

Io vorrei mezzo litro di olio [eeo vorrayee metzo leetro dee olyo]

Please check
the oil
the tyre pressure

the water.

Prego controlli [praygo kontrollee]
il livello dell'olio [eel leevello dellolyo]
la pressione delle gomme [la pressyone dellay gommay]
l'acqua. [lakwa]

Breakdown and accident

I have
  a flat tyre

  had an accident.

Io ho [ee-o o]
  un guasto (alle gomme)
  [oon **gwas**to (**al**lay **gom**may)]
  un incidente. [oon eencheed**en**tay]

Could you give me a lift

  to the nearest petrol station

  to a garage?

Per favore mi dia un passaggio fino
[pair fa**vo**ray mee **dee**a oon pas**saj**jo **fee**no]
  al prossimo distributore di benzina
  [al **pros**seemo deestreeboo**to**ray dee bend**zee**na]
  ad un'officina. [ad oonoffee**chee**na]

Could you
  tow my car away
  help me (push)

  help me jump-start my car

  lend me some petrol
  lend me your jack

  call for a breakdown truck

  call the police/fire brigade

  call an ambulance

  call a doctor?

Per favore può [pair fa**vo**ray pwo]
  rimorchiarmi [reemork**yar**may]
  aiutarmi (spingere)
  [ayoo**tar**mee (**speen**jairay)]
  aiutarmi a partire con la sua batteria
  [ayoo**tar**mee a par**tee**ray kon la **soo**-a battai**ree**a]
  prestarmi benzina [pres**tar**mee bend**zee**na]
  prestarmi il cricco
  [pres**tar**mee eel **kree**ko]
  informare il servizio di soccorso stradale
  [eenfor**ma**ray eel sair**veets**yo dee
  so**kor**so stra**da**lay]
  chiamare la polizia/i pompieri
  [kya**ma**ray la po**leets**eea/ee pomp**yai**ree]
  chiamare una autoambulanza
  [kya**ma**ray **oo**na owtoamboo**lan**tsa]
  chiamare un medico? [kya**ma**ray oon **med**eeko]

Are you injured?
Nobody is injured.

Somebody is (seriously)
injured.

È ferito? [ay fai**ree**to]
Non c'è nessuno ferito.
[non chay nes**soo**no fai**ree**to]
C'è qualcuno ferito (grave).
[chay kwal**koo**no fai**ree**to (**gra**vay)]

Car, motorbike, bicycle

air-conditioning	aria condizionata [aarya kondeetsyonata]
battery	batteria [battaireea]
bicycle tyre	copertone per bicicletta [kopairtonay pair beecheeklaytta]
brake	freno [frayno]
car key	chiave della macchina [kyavay della makkeena]
catalytic converter	catalizzatore [kataleetzatoray]
chain	catena [katayna]
child seat	sedile per bambini [sedeelay pair bambeenee]
engine	motore [motoray]
exhaust	tubo di scarico [toobo dee skareeko]
fan belt	cinghia [cheengya]
first-aid kit	materiale di pronto soccorso [matairyalay dee pronto sokorso]
fuse	valvola di sicurezza [valvola dee seekooretza]
gearshift	cambio [kambyo]
handbrake	freno a mano [frayno a mano]
headlights	faro [faro]/luce anteriore [loochay antairyoray]
horn	clacson [klakson]
light bulb	lampadina [lampadeena]
pump	pompa dell'aria [pompa dellarya]
puncture repair kit	arnesi da rappezzo [arnayzee da rapetzo]
radiator	radiatore [radyatoray]
rear light	luce posteriore [loochay postairyoray]
repair	riparazione [reeparatsyonay]
screw	vite [veetay]
screwdriver	cacciavite [kachaveetay]
seat belt	cintura di sicurezza [cheentoora dee seekooraytza]
spare part	pezzo di ricambio [petzo dee reekambyo]
spare tyre	ruota di scorta [roo-ota dee skorta]
spark plugs	candela di accensione [kandayla dee achensyonay]
steering	sterzo [stairtso]
tank	serbatoio [sairbatoyo]
tools	arnese da lavoro [arnayzay da lavoro]
tow rope	cavo da rimorchio [kavo da reemorkyo]
tube	gomma [gomma]
tyre	ruota [roo-ota]
valve	valvola [valvola]
warning triangle	triangolo di avvertimento [treeangolo dee avairteemanto]
windscreen wipers	tergicristallo [tairjeekreestallo]

Give me . . ., please.
your name and address

your insurance number

Prego mi dia [praygo mee **dee**-a]
il Suo nome e indirizzo
[eel **soo**-o **no**may ay eendee**ree**tzo]
il Suo numero di assicurazione.
[eel **soo**-o **noo**mairo dee asseekoorats**yo**nay]

I was/You were/He was
driving too fast

driving too close.

Io sono/Lei è/Lui è [**ee**-o sono/lay ay /**loo**-ee ay]
andato troppo veloce
[an**da**to **trop**po vaylo**chay**]
andato troppo vicino.
[an**da**to **trop**po veeche**eno**]

I/You/He

ignored the right of way

went through a red light.

Io non ho/Lei non ha/Lui non ha
[**ee**-o non o/lay non a/**loo**-ee non a]
rispettato la precedenza
[reespet**ta**to la preche**den**tsa]
visto la luce rossa [**vee**sto la **loo**chay **ros**sa]

Did you witness the accident?

Lei è testimone dell'incidente?
[lay ay testee**mo**nay delleenchee**den**tay]

Thank you very much for
your help.

Molte grazie per il Suo aiuto.
[**mol**tay **grats**yay pair eel **soo**-o a**yoo**to]

Garage

Where's the nearest (Fiat)
garage?

C'è qui un'officina (per la Fiat)?
[chay kwee oonoffee**chee**na (pair la **fee**-at)]

The engine
won't start
is losing oil
isn't working.

Il motore [eel mo**to**ray]
non parte [non **par**tay]
perde olio [**pair**day **o**lyo]
non funziona bene. [non foonts**yo**na **bay**nay]

The brakes don't work.

I freni non sono in ordine.
[ee **fray**nee non **so**no een **or**deenay]

The warning light is on.

La lampada di controllo è accesa.
[la **lam**pada dee kon**trol**lo ay a**chay**za]

The exhaust/radiator is
leaking/is faulty.

Il tubo di scarico/Il radiatore non è
impermeabile/è difettoso.
[eel **too**bo dee **ska**reeko/eel radya**tor**ay non ay
eempairmaya**bee**lay/ay deefet**to**zo]

How much will the repairs be?

Quanto costa la riparazione?
[**kwan**to **ko**sta la reeparats**yo**nay]

When will the car be ready?

Quando è pronta la macchina?
[**kwan**do ay **pron**ta la **mak**keena]

Hitchhiking

Are you going to . . .?
Could you give me a lift
to . . .?

Lei va a . . .? [lay va a]
Può darmi un passaggio?
[pwo **dar**mee oon pas**saj**jo]

I'd like to get out here, please!
Thanks for the lift!

Vorrei scendere qui! [vor**ray**ee **shen**dairay kwee]
Grazie per il passaggio! [**grats**yay pair eel pas**saj**jo]

Public transport

Bus, tram and underground

Is there a bus to ...?
C'è un autobus per ...? [chay oon **ow**toboos pair]

How long does it take?
Quanto dura il viaggio?
[**kwan**to **doo**ra eel vyajjo]

Excuse me, where's the nearest
Scusi, dov'è la prossima
[**skoo**zee, do**vay** la **pross**ema]

bus stop
fermata dell'autobus [fair**ma**ta dell**ow**toboos]

tram stop
fermata del tram [fair**ma**ta del tram]

underground station?
stazione della metropolitana?
[stats**yo**nay **del**la metropolee**ta**na]

... goes to ...?
... va a ...? [va a]

Which bus
Quale autobus [**kwa**lay **ow**toboos]

Which tram
Quale tram [**kwa**lay tram]

Which tube line
Quale metropolitana [**kwa**lay metropolee**ta**na]

When does the last bus leave?
Quando ritorna l'ultimo autobus?
[**kwan**do ree**tor**na **lool**teemo **ow**toboos]

Does this bus go to...?
È questo l'autobus per ...?
[ay **kwes**to **low**toboos pair]

Where do I have to
Dove devo [do**vay day**vo]

get off
scendere [**shen**dairay]

change for ...
cambiare per ... [kamb**yar**ay pair]

change
cambiare [kamb**yar**ay]

to get to the station
per la stazione [pair la stats**yo**nay]

to get to the airport
per l'aeroporto [pair la-ayro**por**to]

to get to the ... Hotel
per l'albergo ... [pair lal**bair**go]

to get to the city centre?
per il centro? [pair eel **chen**tro]

Could you tell me when I have to get off, please.
Per favore, mi dica quando devo scendere.
[pair fa**vo**ray mee **dee**ka **kwan**do **day**vo **shen**dairay]

A ticket to ..., please.
Un biglietto per ..., prego.
[oon beel**yet**to pair ... **pray**go]

How much is it?
Quanto costa il biglietto per ...?
[**kwan**to **kos**ta eel beel**yet**to pair]

Could you stop here, please!
Prego faccia una fermata qui!
[**pray**go **fa**cha **oo**na fair**ma**ta kwee]

Taxi

Where's the nearest taxi rank?
Dov'è la prossima stazione dei taxi?
[do**vay** la **pross**eema stats**yo**nay **day**ee **ta**xee]

Can you take me ...please?
Mi porti per favore [mee **por**tee pair fa**vo**ray]

to the station
alla stazione [**al**la stats**yo**nay]

to the hotel
all'albergo [allal**bair**go]

to the airport
all'aeroporto [alla-ayro**por**to]

to the centre of town
al centro [al **chen**tro]

to ...
a ... [a]

Signs

Acqua (non) potabile (not) drinking water!	**Lavabo** washroom
Banchina platform	**Libero** free
Binario platform	**Occupato** occupied
Freno d'allarme emergency brake	**Uscita** exit
Gabinetti toilets	**Vagone cuccette** couchette
Informazioni information	**Vagone letto** sleeper/sleeping car
	Vagone ristorante dining car

How much is it to ...?
Quanto costa il viaggio per ...?
[**kwan**to **kos**ta eel **vyaj**jo pair]

Could you switch on the meter, please?
Inserisca per favore il tassametro.
[eensai**rees**ka pair fa**vor**ay eel **tas**sametro]

Could you stop here, please.
Si fermi qui prego.
[see **fair**mee kwee **pray**go]

That's for you!
Questo è per Lei! [**kwes**to ay pair lay]

Getting around by train and bus

Where's the (bus) station, please?
Scusi, dov'è la stazione (dei pullman)?
[**skoo**zee do**vay** la stats**yo**nay (**day**ee **pool**man)]

When's the next train/ bus to ...?
Quando parte un treno/pullman per ...?
[**kwan**do **par**tay oon **tray**no/**pool**man pair]

Do I have to change?
Devo scendere? [**day**vo **shen**dairay]

Which platform does the train leave from?
Da quale binario parte il treno?
[da **kwa**lay beena**ree**o **par**tay eel **tray**no]

When does the train/bus arrive in ...?
Quando arriva il treno/pullman a ...?
[**kwan**do ar**ree**va eel **tray**no/**pool**man a]

Is there a connection to ... in ...?
C'è una coincidenza a ... per ...?
[chay **oo**na koeenchee**den**tsa a ... pair]

How much is it?
Quanto costa il viaggio?
[**kwan**to **kos**ta eel **vyaj**jo]

Are there special rates for children?
C'è uno sconto per bambini?
[chay **oo**no **skon**to pair bam**bee**nee]

A ... ticket/tickets, please
Prego un biglietto/dei biglietti
[**pray**go oon beel**yet**to/**day**ee beel**yet**tee]

  to ...
    per ... [pair]

    single/return
      semplice/andata e ritorno
      [**sem**pleechay/an**da**ta ay ree**tor**no]

    first-class/second-class
      prima/seconda classe
      [**pree**ma/se**kon**da **klas**say]

    for two adults and two children.
      per due adulti e due bambini.
      [pair **doo**ay a**dool**tee ay **doo**ay bam**bee**nee]

I'd like to book ...	**Prego riservi per il treno/per l'autobus per ...**
on the train/bus to ...	[**pray**go ree**sair**vee pair eel **tray**no/pair lowto**boos** pair]
a (window) seat	un posto vicino alla finestra
	[oon **pos**to vee**chee**no **al**la fee**nes**tra]
a non- smoker/smoker	non fumatori/fumatori
seat	[non fooma**tor**ee/fooma**tor**ee]
a couchette	un posto cuccetta [oon **pos**to koo**chet**ta]
a sleeper.	un posto vagone letto.
	[oon **pos**to vago**nay let**to]
on the two o'clock train/bus	alle ore quattordici [**al**lay **o**ray kwat**tor**deechee]

I'd like	**Io vorrei** [ee-o vor**ray**ee]
to take my bycicle with me.	portare la mia bicicletta
	[por**tar**ay la **mee**-a beechee**klet**ta]
to check in my luggage.	consegnare questo pacco.
	[konsen**yar**ay **kwes**to **pak**ko]

Where can I find	**Scusi, dove trovo** [**skoo**zee, **do**vay **tro**vo]
the information desk	lo sportello per le informazioni
	[lo spor**tel**lo pair lay eenformats**yo**nee]
the left-luggage office	il deposito bagagli [eel de**pos**eeto ba**gal**yee]
the lockers	la cassetta di custodia?
	[la kas**set**ta dee koos**to**deea]
Is this the train/bus to ...?	È questo il treno/l'autobus per ...?
	[ay **kwes**to eel **tray**no/lowto**boos** pair]
Is this seat taken, please?	**Scusi, è libero questo posto?**
	[**skoo**zee ay **lee**bairo **kwes**to **pos**to]

Getting around by plane

I'd like to	**Io vorrei** [ee-o vor**ray**ee]
to book a flight to ...	riservare un volo per ...
	[reesair**var**ay oon **vo**lo pair]
for 1 person/2 people	per una persona/due persone
	[pair **oo**na pair**so**na/**doo**ay pair**so**nay]
on ...	il ... [eel]
one-way/return	semplice/andata e volo di ritorno
	[**sem**pleechay/an**da**ta ay **vo**lo dee ree**tor**no]
economy class/first class.	classe turistica/prima classe
	[**klas**say too**rees**teeka/**pree**ma **klas**say]
to confirm a flight	confermare un volo [konfair**mar**ay oon **vo**lo]
to cancel/change the flight.	stornare/prenotare per un altro volo.
	[stor**nar**ay/preno**tar**ay pair oon **al**tro **vo**lo]

Where is	**Dov'è** [do**vay**]
terminal 1/2/3	il terminale uno/due/tre
	[eel tairmee**na**lay **oo**no/**doo**ay/tray]
the information desk?	lo sportello per le informazioni?
	[lo spor**tel**lo pair lay eenformats**yo**nee]
When does the plane from ...	Quando atterra l'aereo da ...?
arrive?	[**kwan**do at**tair**ra la-**ay**rayo da]

30

Are there any seats ... left?
Ci sono ancora posti liberi
[chee **so**no an**ko**ra **pos**tee **lee**bairee]

  by the window/aisle
  vicino alla finestra/al corridoio
  [vee**chee**no **al**la fee**nes**tra/al korree**do**yo]

  smoking/non-smoking
  per fumatori/non fumatori?
  [pair fooma**to**ree/non fooma**to**ree]

How much is the ticket?
Quanto costa il volo? [**kwan**to **kos**ta eel **vo**lo]

Are there any special rates/
stand-by seats?
Ci sono tariffe speciali/posti stand by?
[chee **so**no ta**reef**fay spe**cha**lee/**pos**tee stand by]

When do I have to be at the
airport?
Quando devo essere all'aeroporto?
[**kwan**do **day**vo **es**sairay alla-airo**por**to]

How much is the airport tax?
Quant'è la tariffa per l'aeroporto?
[**kwan**tay la ta**reef**fa pair la-airo**por**to]

My suitcase/My bag
La mia valigia/La mia borsa
[la **mee**-a va**lee**ja/la **mee**-a **bor**sa]

  has been damaged
  è danneggiata [ay dannay**ja**ta]

  is missing.
  è sparita. [ay spa**ree**ta]

Getting around by boat

When does the next boat/(car)
ferry leave for ...?
Quando parte una nave/un traghetto per ...?
[**kwan**do **par**tay **oo**na **na**vay/oon tra**get**to pair]

How long does the crossing
take?
Quanto dura la traversata?
[**kwan**to **doo**ra la travair**sa**ta]

I'd like
Io vorrei [**ee**-o vor**ray**ee]

  a ticket to ...
  un biglietto per ... [oon beel**yet**to pair]

    first class/tourist class
    prima/seconda classe
    [**pree**ma/se**kon**da **klas**say]

    reclining seats
    sedile a sdraio [se**dee**lay a **zdra**yo]

    a single cabin
    una cabina singola [**oo**na ka**bee**na **seen**gola]

    a double cabin
    una cabina doppia [**oo**na ka**bee**na **dop**ya]

    an outside/inside cabin.
    una cabina esterna/interna.
    [**oo**na ka**bee**na es**tair**na/een**tair**na]

I'd like to take the car
with me.
Io vorrei portare la mia auto.
[**ee**-o vor**ray**ee por**ta**ray la **mee**-a **ow**to]

When do I/we have to be
on board?
Quando devo/dobbiamo stare a bordo?
[**kwan**do **day**vo/dobb**ya**mo **sta**ray a **bor**do]

When do we arrive at ...?
Quando ancoriamo a ...?
[**kwan**do ankor**eea**mo a]

How long are we stopping
for?
Per quanto tempo ci fermiamo?
[pair **kwan**to **tem**po chee fair**mya**mo]

I'm looking for
Io cerco [**ee**-o **chair**ko]

  cabin number ...
  la cabina numero ... [la ka**bee**na **noo**mairo]

  the restaurant
  il ristorante [eel reesto**ran**tay]

  the shop
  un negozio [oon ne**gots**yo]

  the toilets
  i gabinetti [ee gabee**net**tee]

  the parking deck
  il ponte di parcheggio [eel **pon**tay dee par**kay**jo]

  a steward.
  un cameriere di bordo.
  [oon kamairee**yai**ray dee **bor**do]

31

Among the vineyards of Chianti you can relax in style in a traditional country house

Accommodation

Hotel and guesthouse

Where can I find
a good/cheap hotel

a guesthouse
close to the beach
in the centre of town
in a quiet location?

Where is the ... hotel/
guesthouse?

C'è ... qui vicino [chay kwee veecheeno]
un albergo buono/semplice
[oon albairgo bwono sempleechay]
una pensione [oona pensyonay]
vicino alla spiaggia [veecheeno alla spyajja]
nel centro [nel chentro]
in un posto tranquillo
[een oon posto trankweello]

Dov'è l'albergo/la pensione ...?
[dovay lalbairgo/la pensyonay]

At the reception desk

I have a reservation.

My name is ...

Io ho fatto riservare una camera.
[ee-o o fatto reesairvaray oona kamaira]
Il mio nome è ... [eel mee-o nomay ay]

Have you got any vacancies
for 1 night
for 1 day
for 2/3 days
for 1 week?

Ha una camera libera [a oona kamaira leebaira]
per una notte [pair oona nottay]
per un giorno [pair oon jorno]
per due/tre giorni [pair dooay/tray jornee]
per una settimana? [pair oona setteemana]

* Noi siamo purtroppo al
completo. [noy syamo
poortroppo al komplayto]

I'm afraid we're fully booked.

There's a vacancy from ...

Dal... ci sarà qualcosa libero.
[dal... chee sara kwalkoza leebairo]

I'd like/We'd like

Io vorrei/Noi vorremmo
[**ee**-o vor**ray**ee/noy vor**ray**mo]

a room with a shower
    una camera con doccia
    [**oo**na **ka**maira kon **do**cha]

a single room
    una camera singola [**oo**na **ka**maira **seen**gola]
a double room
    una camera doppia [**oo**na **ka**maira **dop**ya]
a room with twin beds
    una camera a due letti
    [**oo**na **ka**maira a **doo**ay **let**tee]

    with a bath and toilet
      con bagno e gabinetto
      [**kon ban**yo ay gabee**net**to]

    with a balcony
      con balcone [kon bal**kon**ay]
    facing the beach/at the
    front.
      sulla spiaggia/sulla strada.
      [**sool**la spyaj**ja**/**sool**la **stra**da]

How much is the room

Quanto costa la camera
[**kwan**to **kos**ta la **ka**maira]

per person
    a persona [a pair**so**na]
per night
    per notte [pair **not**tay]
per week
    per settimana [pair settee**ma**na]
    with/without breakfast
      con/senza colazione [kon/**sen**dza kolat**syo**nay]
    with half board
      con mezza pensione [kon **met**za pen**syo**nay]
    with full board
      con pensione completa
      [kon pen**syo**nay kom**play**ta]

    for children?
      per bambini? [pair bam**bee**nee]

Does the room have a
television/telephone?
La camera è con televisione/telefono?
[la **ka**maira ay kon telayvee**zyo**nay/te**lay**fono]

I'd like to see the room.
Vorrei vedere la camera.
[vor**ray**ee ve**dair**ay la **ka**maira]

This room is nice/is O.K.
La camera è bella/in ordine.
[la **ka**maira ay **bel**la/een **or**deenay]

I don't like this room.
La camera non mi piace.
[la **ka**maira non mee **pya**chay]

Do you have another room?
Ha un'altra camera?
[a oo**nal**tra **ka**maira]

Can I pay by cheque/credit
card?
Posso pagare con assegno/carta di credito?
[**pos**so pa**gar**ay kon as**sen**yo/**kar**ta dee **kray**deeto]

Do you have
  a car park
  a (supervised) garage

Avete [a**vay**tay]
  un parcheggio [oon par**kay**jo]
  un garage (sorvegliato)
  [oon ga**raj** (sorvel**ya**to)]
  a safe
    una cassaforte [**oo**na kassa**for**tay]
  a swimming-pool?
    una piscina [**oo**na pee**shee**na]
  a sauna
    una sauna [**oo**na sa**oo**na]
  your own beach?
    una spiaggia propria?
    [**oo**na spyaj**ja prop**reea]

Where is
  the breakfast room

Dov'è [do**vay**]
  il posto per la colazione
  [eel **pos**to pair la kolat**syo**nay]
  the dining room?
    la sala da pranzo? [la **sa**la da **pran**dzo]

ACCOMMODATION

What time is
breakfast
lunch/dinner?

Quando è l'ora di [kwando ay lora dee]
colazione [kolatsyonay]
pranzo/cena? [**prandzo/chay**na]

▶ (Food and Drink, see page 40)

Would you wake me
tomorrow at 7, please!

Mi svegli domani alle sette per piacere!
[mee **svay**lyee do**ma**nee **al**lay **set**tay pair
peea**chair**ay]

My key, please!

La mia chiave, per favore!
[la **mee**-a **kya**voray pair fa**vor**ay]

Room number 10, please!

Camera numero dieci prego!
[**ka**maira **noo**mairo **dyay**chee **pray**go]

Where can I
change money
cash traveller's cheques

buy stamps/postcards

make a phone call?

È possibile [ay posseebeelay]
cambiare soldi [kam**byar**ay **sol**dee]
riscuotere traveller's cheques [reesk**wot**airay
travellers sheks]
comprare francobolli/cartoline
[kom**prar**ay franko**bol**lee/karto**lee**nay]
telefonare? [telayfo**nar**ay]

Can I make a phone call to
England from my room?

Posso telefonare dalla mia camera in Inghilterra?
[**pos**so telayfo**nar**ay **dal**la **mee**-a **ka**maira een
eengeel**tair**a]

Please put me through to
the following number ...!

Mi può collegare con il numero ... per favore?
[mee pwo kolle**gar**ay kon eel **noo**mairo ... pair
fa**vor**ay]

Are there any letters for me?

C'è posta per me? [chay **pos**ta pair may]

Complaints

The room is dirty/too loud.

La camera è sporca/rumorosa.
[la **ka**maira ay **spor**ka/roomoro**za**]

There's no (hot) water.

Noi non abbiamo acqua (calda).
[noy non ab**by**amo akwa (**kal**da)]

... does not work.
The light
The shower
The toilet
The heating

... non funziona. [non foontsyona]
La luce [la **loo**chay]
La doccia [la do**cha**]
Il gabinetto [eel gabee**net**to]
Il riscaldamento [eel reeskalda**men**to]

There are no
towels
hangers.
There is no toilet paper.

Mancano [**man**kano]
asciugamani [ashooga**ma**nee]
grucce [**groo**chay]
Manca carta igienica [**man**ka **kar**ta eejye**nee**ka]

Could we have (another)

blanket
pillow?

Noi abbiamo (ancora) bisogno di
[noy ab**by**amo (an**ko**ra) bee**zon**yo dee]
una coperta [**oo**na ko**pair**ta]
un cuscino. [oon koo**shee**no]

I've lost the key to my room.

Io ho perso la mia chiave della camera.
[ee-o o **pair**so la **mee**-a **kya**vay **del**la **ka**maira]

34

Hotel reservation by fax

Hotel Lungomare
Salerno
FAX ...

Gentili Signore e Signori,

io vorrei/noi vorremmo prenotare dal 1 al 15 agosto 2001 una camera per 1/2 persone, si e possibile con doccia e balcone. Prego mi/ci informi dei prezzi per camera singola/camera doppia con colazione/mezza pensione/pensione completa e mi/ci informi subito sull'effettuato prenotamento.

Distinti saluti.

Hotel Lungomare
Salerno
FAX ...

Dear sir,

I/We would like to reserve a room from 1 to 15 August 2001 for one/two persons, if possible with shower and balcony. Please let me/us know the price for a single/double room with breakfast/half-board/full board so that I/we can confirm my/our booking as soon as possible.

Best wishes

Departure

I'm leaving/We're leaving tomorrow/today.	Io parto/Noi partiamo domani/oggi. [ee-o **par**to/noy part**ya**mo do**ma**nee/**oj**jee]
I'd like my bill, please.	Il conto prego. [eel **kon**to **pray**go]
Would you call a taxi for me, please.	Chiami per favore un taxi. [**kya**mee pair fa**vor**ay oon **tax**ee]
It's been very nice here.	A noi è piaciuto molto qui. [a noy ay peea**choo**to **mol**to kwee]
Thank you very much!	Molte grazie! [**mol**tay **grats**yay]
Good-bye.	Arrivederci. [arreevay**dair**chee]

Holiday cottage and holiday flat

We're looking for
  a holiday cottage

  a holiday flat

  a (quiet) holiday flat

    for 2/4 people
    for 6 days/2 weeks.

How many rooms does the flat have?

How much is the cottage?

Are there any additional costs?

Are pets/dogs allowed?

Noi cerchiamo [noy chair**kya**mo]
  una casa per le vacanze
  [**oo**na **ka**za pair le va**kant**say]
  un appartamento per le vacanze
  [oon apparta**men**to pair lay va**kant**say]
  un appartamento (tranquillo)
  [oon apparta**men**to (trank**weel**lo)]
    per 2/4 persone [pair **doo**ay/**kwat**tro pairsonay]
    per sei giorni/due settimane.
    [pair **say**ee **jor**nee/**doo**ay sette**ma**nay]

Quante camere ha l'appartamento [**kwan**tay kamairay a lapparta**men**to]
Quanto costa la casa [**kwan**to **kos**ta la **ka**za]
Le spese accessorie sono da pagare a parte?
[lay **spay**zay ach**essor**yay **so**no da paga**ray** a **par**tay]
Sono permessi animali domestici/cani?
[**so**no pair**mess**ee anee**ma**lee do**mays**teechee/**ka**nee]

35

Do we have to clean it before we leave?

Dobbiamo fare noi le pulizie finali?
[dobbyamo **far**ay noy lay pool**eets**yay feen**a**lee]

Where can I
go shopping
make a phone call
do the laundry?

Dove si può [**do**vay see pwo]
fare la spesa [**far**ay la **spay**za]
telefonare [telayfo**nar**ay]
lavare biancheria? [la**var**ay beeankai**ree**a]

Camping

Have you got room for
a tent
a caravan
a camper van?

Avete posto per [a**vay**tay **pos**to pair]
una tenda [**oo**na **ten**da]
una roulotte [**oo**na roo**lott**]
un camper? [oon **kam**pair]

What's the charge

for one person
for a car
for a camper van
for a caravan
for a tent?

Quanto costa il posto
[**kwan**to **kos**ta eel **pos**to]
a persona [a pair**so**na]
per una macchina [pair **oo**na **mak**keena]
per un camper [pair oon **kam**pair]
per una roulotte [pair **oo**na roo**lott**]
per una tenda? [pair **oo**na **ten**da]

Do you also rent out
caravans
tents
bungalows/cabins?

Affitta anche [af**feet**ta an**kay**]
roulotte [roo**lott**]
tende [**ten**day]
villini/capanne? [veel**lee**nee/ka**pan**nay]

Where are the showers/ toilets?

Dove sono le docce/i gabinetti?
[**do**vay **so**no lay **doch**ay/ee gabee**net**tee]

We need

a power point

a tap for water

a sewerage connection.

Noi abbiamo bisogno di un
[**no**-ee abb**ya**mo beezon**yo** dee oon]
collegamento per la corrente
[kolle**gamen**to pair la kor**ren**tay]
collegamento per l'acqua
[kolle**gamen**to pair **lak**wa]
collegamento alla canalizzazione.
[kolle**gamen**to alla kanaleetzats**yo**naye]

When is the gate locked at night?
Is the camp-site guarded at night?

Quando viene chiuso il portone di notte?
[**kwan**do vyay**nay kyoo**zo eel por**to**nay dee **not**tay]
Il posto è sorvegliato di notte?
[eel **pos**to ay sorvel**ya**to dee **not**tay]

Does the camp-site have

a supermarket
washing machines

cool boxes

a playground?

C'è al campeggio
[chay al kam**pay**jo]
un supermercato [oon soopairmair**ka**to]
una lavatrice a gettoni
[**oo**na lava**tree**chay a **jet**tonee]
un frigorifero da affittare
[oon freego**ree**fairo da affeet**tar**ay]
un parco giochi? [oon **par**ko **jok**ee]

Youth Hostel

Is there a youth hostel around here?	C'è un ostello della gioventù qui vicino? [chay oon ostello della joventoo kwee veecheeno]
How much is it per night per person (with breakfast)?	Quanto costa un pernottamento a persona (con colazione)? [kwanto kosta oon pairnottamento a pairsona (kon kolatsyonay)]
I/We will stay for two days/ weeks.	Io rimango/Noi rimaniamo due giorni/ settimane. [ee-o reemango/noy reemanyamo dooay jornee/setteemanay]

Accommodation

adapter	spina di riduzione [speena dee reedootsyonay]
air-conditioning	aria condizionata [arya kondeetsyonata]
apartment	appartamento [appartamento]
ashtray	portacenere [portachaynairay]
balcony	balcone [balkonay]
bathtub	vasca da bagno [vaska da banyo]
bed	letto [letto]
bedlinen	lenzuola e coperte [lenzwola e kopairtay]
bill	conto [konto]
blanket	coperta da letto [kopairta da letto]
bottled gas	bombola di gas [bombola dee gaz]
camper van	camper [kampair]
caravan	roulotte [roolott]
car park	parcheggio [parkayjo]
chambermaid	cameriera [kamaireeyaira]
change	spiccioli *(m/Pl)* [speecholee]
clean	pulire [pooleeray]
coat hanger	gruccia [groocha]
coffee machine	caffettiera [kaffetyaira]
coin	moneta [monayta]
cooker	cucina [koocheena]
cot	letto per bambini [letto pair bambeenee]
crockery	piatti [peeattee]
dining room	sala da pranzo [sala da prandzo]
drinking water	acqua potabile [akwa potabeelay]
electricity	corrente elettrica [korrentay elayttreeka]
extra costs	spese accessorie [spayzay achessoryay]
family room	camera per famiglia [kamaira pair fameelya]
fan	ventilatore [vaynteelatoray]
final cleaning	pulizie finali [pooleetsyay feenalee]
garage	garage [garaj]
guesthouse	pensione [pensyonay]
heating	riscaldamento [reeskaldamento]

I need/I don't need bedlinen.   Io (non) ho bisogno di lenzuola e coperte.
[ee-o (non) o beezonyo dee lenzwola ay kopairtay]

When is the front door
locked?   Quando viene chiusa la porta di entrata?
[kwando vyaynay kyooza la porta dee entrata]

How far is it to   **Quanto è lontano fino**
[kwanto ay lontano feeno]

    the beach   alla spiaggia [alla spyajja]
    the town centre   in città [een cheetta]
    the station?   alla stazione? [alla statsyonay]

hire	noleggiare [nolayjaray]
hire charge	tassa di noleggio [tassa dee nolayjo]
kitchen	cucina [koocheena]
key	chiave [kyavay]
lift	ascensore [ashensoray]
light	luce [loochay]
luggage	bagaglio [bagalyo]
pillow	cuscino [kusheeno]
pots	pentole [pentolay]
power point	collegamento elettrico [kollegamento elayttreeko]
radio	radio [radyo]
reduction	riduzione [reedootsyonay]
repair	riparare [reepararay]
rubbish	spazzatura [spatzatoora]
rubbish bin	secchio per la spazzatura [sekyo pair la spatzatoora]
safe	cassaforte [kassafortay]
shower	doccia [docha]
sink	lavandino [lavandeeno]
sleeping bag	sacco a pelo [sakko a paylo]
soap	sapone [saponay]
sports ground	campo sportivo [kampo sporteevo]
tea towel	straccio per i piatti [stracho pair ee peeattee]
television	televisore [telayveezoray]
telephone	telefono [telayfono]
tent peg	picchetto [peeketto]
toilet	gabinetto [gabeenetto]
toilet paper	carta igienica [karta eejayneeka]
towel	asciugamano [ashoogamano]
wash	lavare [lavaray]
washing machine	lavatrice [lavatreechay]
water	acqua [akwa]

There is nearly always somewhere nearby that sells ice-cream and a cool drink

Food and Drink

Is there ... around here?

C'é ... qui vicino
[chay ... kwee vee**chee**no]

a good restaurant
un buon ristorante [oon bw**on** reesto**ran**tay]

a reasonably cheap restaurant
un ristorante economico
[oon reesto**ran**tay ekono**mee**ko]

a nice/a typical restaurant
un locale carino/tipico
[oon lo**ka**lay ka**ree**no/**tee**peeko]

with regional/ international cuisine?
con cucina nostrana/internazionale
[kon koo**chee**na nos**tra**na/eentairnatsyo**na**lay]

I'd like/We'd like

Io vorrei/Noi vorremmo
[ee-o vor**ray**ee/noy vor**ray**mo]

to have breakfast
fare colazione [**far**ay kolats**yo**nay]

to have lunch/dinner
pranzare/cenare [pran**tza**ray/che**nar**ay]

a snack
mangiare una piccolezza
[man**jar**ay **oo**na peeko**lay**tza]

just something to drink.
solo bere qualcosa. [**so**lo **bair**ray kwal**ko**za]

I'd like to reserve a table

Io vorrei ordinare un tavolo
[ee-o vor**ray**ee ordee**nar**ay oon **ta**volo]

for tonight/tomorrow night
per oggi/domani sera
[pair **oj**jee/do**ma**nee **sai**ra]

at 7/8 o'clock
alle ore diciannove/venti
[**al**lay **or**ay deechan**no**vay/**ven**tee]

for 4/6.
per quattro/sei persone
[payr **kwat**tro/**say**ee pair**so**nay]

The name is ...
a nome di ... [a **no**may dee]

I've reserved a table. The name is ...
Io ho ordinato un tavolo a nome di ...
[ee-o o ordee**na**to oon **ta**volo a **no**may dee]

40

A table for 2/4, please! | Un tavolo per due/quattro persone prego!
[oon **ta**volo pair **doo**ay/**kwat**tro pair**so**nay **pray**go]

Is this table/seat taken? | Questo tavolo/posto è libero?
[**kwes**to **ta**volo/**pos**to ay **lee**bairo]

Do you have high chairs? | Avete sedie per bambini?
[a**vay**tay **say**deeay pair bam**bee**nee]

Excuse me, where's the toilet? | Dove sono i gabinetti per favore?
[**do**vay **so**no ee gabee**net**tee pair fa**vor**ay]

How to Order

Excuse me, please! | Cameriere, prego! [kamair**yair**ay **pray**go]
Could I have the menu/menu of the day/list of drinks/wine list/ice-cream menu, please! | Il menù/menù del giorno/menù delle bevande/menù del vino/menù dei gelati prego! [eel me**noo**/me**noo** del **jor**no/me**noo** del**lay** be**van**day/me**noo** del **vee**no/me**noo** **day**ee je**la**tee **pray**go]

What can you recommend? | Che cosa mi consiglia? [kay **ko**za mee kon**seel**ya]

I'll have | **Io vorrei/Io prendo**
[ee-o vor**ray**ee/ee-o **pren**do]

  soup | una zuppa [**oo**na **tsoop**pa]
  the dish of the day | il menù del giorno [eel me**noo** del **jor**no]
  menu number 1/2 | il menù numero uno/due
   | [eel me**noo** **noo**mairo **oo**no/**doo**ay]

  this | questo qui [**kwes**to kwee]
    as a starter/as the main course/for dessert. | come antipasto/piatto principale/dessert.
     | [**ko**may ante**pas**to/**pyat**to preenchee**pa**lay/des**sair**]

Do you have any regional specialities? | Quali sono i piatti tipici della regione?
[**kwa**lee **so**no ee **pyat**tee **tee**peechee **del**la re**jo**nay]

Could I have pasta/rice instead of chips, please? | Io vorrei pasta/riso invece delle patatine fritte.
[ee-o vor**ray**ee **pas**ta/**ree**zo een**vay**chay **del**lay pata**tee**nay **freet**tay]

Breakfast Italian-style

The notion of a family breakfast is alien to most Italian households. Before the children go to school, they are given a glass of warm milk and a few biscuits, but the menfolk will have a drink and a bite to eat on their way to work in one of the many bars which exist throughout Italy, north and south. The order is nearly always a coffee in the form of an *espresso* or *cappuccino*, accompanied by a *cornetto* (croissant).

In Italy, the bar is a meeting place, where people go to exchange news and gossip, pick up their cigarettes or make a phone call. Most Italians have their own favourite bar, where they pop in regularly for breakfast, a quick bite at lunchtime – maybe a slice of pizza or a *panino* (sandwich) – or to watch the football on TV in the evening.

As Italy is not generally well-supplied with public toilets, many people come in off the street to make use of the bar toilets. It is the done thing, however, to order a drink or buy at least something before using the WC.

Coffee the Italian way

An Italian *caffè* is usually served strong, without milk and taken with lots of sugar. If you want something even stronger, then order a *ristretto*, which is a strong *espresso*. A *cappuccino* is a normal *caffè* or *espresso* with a topping of foamy milk and a sprinkling of cocoa. If you want coffee with milk then order a *caffè latte*. It is usually served in a glass or a cup without a handle. An *espresso corretto* has an added shot of brandy.

For the child/children

a small portion
a children's portion

an extra plate
extra cutlery, please.

Do you have a vegetarian dish?

Is this dish (very) hot/sweet/rich?

Per il bambino/i bambini
[pair eel bambeeno/ee bambeenee]
    una porzione piccola [**oo**na ports**yo**nay **pee**kola]
    un piatto per bambini
    [oon pee**at**to pair bam**bee**nee]
    un piatto extra [oon pee**at**to **ex**tra]
    posate extra [po**za**tay **ex**tra]

C'è una pietanza vegetale?
[chay **oo**na peeay**tan**tza veje**ta**lay]

Questa pietanza è (molto) piccante/dolce/grassa? [**kwes**ta peeay**tan**tza ay (**mol**to) peekantay/**dol**chay/**gras**sa]

To drink, I'd like/we'd like

a glass
a bottle
a quarter of a litre
half a litre/one litre of
red/white wine, please.

Do you serve wine in carafes?

Thank you, that's all.

Prego, vorrei/vorremmo
[**pray**go vor**ray**/vor**ray**mo]
    un bicchiere [oon beek**yai**ray]
    una bottiglia [**oo**na bot**tee**lya]
    un quarto [oon **kwar**to]
    mezzo litro/un litro di vino rosso/bianco.
    [**met**zo **lee**tro/oon **lee**tro di **vee**no **ros**so/**byan**ko]

Avete anche vini aperti?
[a**vay**tay **an**kay **vee**nee a**pair**tee]

Grazie, questo è tutto. [**grats**yay **kwes**to ay **toot**to]

Could I have ..., please?
some more bread
another beer

Enjoy your meal!
Cheers!/Your health!

Posso avere ancora [**pos**so a**vai**ray an**ko**ra]
    del pane [del **pa**nay]
    una birra? [**oo**na **beer**ra]

Buon appetito! [**bwon** appay**tee**to]
Salute!/Alla tua/Sua salute!
[sa**loo**tay/alla **too**a/**soo**a sa**loo**tay]

Complaints

That's not what I ordered!

Questo non l'ho ordinato!
[**kwes**to non lo ordee**na**to]

I'm sorry but
the food is cold
the meat is tough/not
cooked through.

Mi dispiace, ma [mee deespyachay ma]
    il cibo è freddo [eel **chee**bo ay **fred**do]
    la carne è dura/non è cotta bene.
    [la **kar**nay ay **doo**ra/non ay **kot**ta **bay**nay]

We still need . . ., please?/ **Could we have . . ., please?**	**Manca ancora/Ci porti ancora** [**man**ka an**ko**ra/chee **por**tee an**ko**ra]
some cutlery	posate [po**za**tay]
another knife/another fork	un coltello/una forchetta [oon kol**tel**lo/**oo**na for**ket**ta]
another tea spoon	un cucchiaino [oon kookya**ee**no]
another plate	un piatto [oon **pyat**to]
another glass	un bicchiere [oon beek**yai**ray]
oil and vinegar	aceto e olio [a**chay**to ay **o**lyo]
salt and pepper	sale e pepe [**sa**lay ay **pay**pay]
an ashtray	un portacenere [**oon** porta**chay**nairay]
napkins	tovaglioli [toval**yo**lee]
toothpicks	stuzzicadenti. [stootzeeka**den**tee]

Have you forgotten my food/drink?	Ha dimenticato la mia pietanza/bevanda? [a deementee**ka**to la **mee**-a peea**tan**tsa/be**van**da]
There seems to be a mistake in the bill	Io credo che il conto non sia preciso. [ee-o **kray**do kay eel **kon**to non seea pre**chee**zo]
What is this, please?	Cosa è questo? [**ko**za ay **kwes**to]
I didn't have that!	Questo non l'ho avuto! [**kwes**to non lo a**voo**to]

Paying the bill

Could I have the bill, please!	Il conto per favore! [eel **kon**to pair fa**vo**ray]
All together, please.	Pago tutto insieme. [**pa**go **too**tto een**syay**may]
Separate bills, please.	Paghiamo separatamente. [pa**gya**mo separata**men**tay]
Could I have a receipt, please?	Vorrei una ricevuta, prego. [vor**ray**ee **oo**na reechay**voo**ta **pray**go]
Did you enjoy the meal?	È piaciuto? [ay peea**choo**to]
Was everything OK?	Sono soddisfatti? [**so**no soddees**fat**tee]
It was very good, thank you.	Grazie, è stato molto buono. [**grats**yay ay **sta**to **mol**to bwono]
That's for you.	Questo è per Lei. [**kwes**to ay pair lay]
Keep the change!	Va bene così! [va **bay**nay ko**zee**]

Traditional Italian fare

If you want to sample authentic Italian food with the atmosphere to match, then go to one of the many *trattorie* or *osterie* where local families eat. These family-run restaurants usually serve regional dishes made with locally-produced ingredients, which are always seasonal. *Trattorie* and *osterie* don't always have signs outside, but wherever you see locals eating, you are more or less guaranteed that the food's going to be good.

If you just want something hot to keep you going, then go to a *rosticceria* or a *tavola calda* (a sort of snack bar). Here you will find the ubiquitous *pizza*, but also *calzone*, a parcel of pastry stuffed with cheese, tomatoes, mushrooms, artichokes or ham fillings and then fried in oil.

43

Food

Colazione	Breakfast
Burro [**boor**ro]	butter
Cacao [ka**ka**o]	cocoa
Caffè [ka**ffay**]	coffee
con dolcificante [kon dolcheefee**kan**tay]	with sweetener
con/senza latte [kon/**sen**dza **lat**tay]	with/without milk
con zucchero [kon **tsoo**kairo]	with sugar
senza caffeina [**sen**dza kaffay-**ee**na]	decaffeinated
Formaggio [for**ma**jjo]	cheese
Jogurt [**yo**goort]	yogurt
Latte (caldo/freddo) [**lat**tay (**kal**do/**fred**do)]	(hot/cold) milk
Marmellata [marmel**la**ta]	jam
Miele [m**yay**lay]	honey
Pane [**pa**nay]	bread
Pane integrale [**pa**nay eente**gra**lay]	wholemeal bread
Panini [pa**nee**nee]	bread roll
Tè [tay]	tea
alla menta [**alla men**ta]	peppermint tea
alle erbe [**allay air**bay]	herbal tea
con limone [kon lee**mo**nay]	with lemon
Toast [**tost**]	toast
Uovo [**wo**vo]	egg
Uovo à la coque [**wo**vo a la kok]	soft boiled egg

Merende	Snacks
Panino [pa**nee**no]	sandwich
Toast [**tost**]	toast
con formaggio [kon for**ma**jjo]	with cheese
con prosciutto [kon pro**shoot**to]	with ham
con salame [kon sa**la**may]	with salami

Antipasti	Starters
Antipasto misto [antee**pas**to **mees**to]	mixed starters
Antipasto nostrano [antee**pas**to no**stra**no]	starters recommended by the chef
Caprese [ka**pray**zay]	tomatoes with mozzarella
Cocktail di gamberetti [**kok**ta-eel dee gambay**ret**tee]	prawn cocktail
Crostini di funghi [kro**stee**nee dee **foon**gee]	stuffed mushrooms on toasted bread
Giardiniera [jardeen**yai**ra]	mixed marinated vegetables
Insalata di frutti di mare [insa**la**ta dee **froot**tee dee **mar**ay]	seafood salad
Lumache [loo**ma**kay]	snails

Minestre	Soups
Brodo (con uovo) [**bro**do (kon oo-**o**vo)]	clear soup (with egg)
Minestrone [meene**stro**nay]	vegetable soup
Pastina in brodo [pa**stee**na een **bro**do]	noodle soup
Stracciatella [stracha**tel**la]	clear soup with beaten egg

Pasta e riso

Cannelloni ripieni [kannellonee reepyaynee]	stuffed cannelloni
Fettuccine ai quattro formaggi [fettoocheenay a-ee kwattro formajjee]	fettuccine with four different types of cheese
Fettuccine alla Fiorentina [fettoocheenay alla feeorenteena]	fettuccine with spinach
Maccheroni ai calamari [makkaironee a-ee kalamaree]	macaroni with squid sauce
Penne al pomodoro [pennay al pomodoro]	penne with tomato sauce
Ravioli [raveeolee]	ravioli
Rigatoni alla Carrettiera [reegatonee alla karrettyaira]	rigatoni with meat, tuna and mushrooms
Rigatoni alla contadina [reegatonee alla kontadeena]	rigatoni with tomatoes, olives and capers
Risi e bisi [reezee ay beezee]	rice with peas
Risotto alla milanese [reezotto alla meelanayzay]	regional rice dish with saffron
Spaghetti [spagettee]	spaghetti
all'amatriciana [allamatreechana]	with tomato sauce and bacon
alla bolognese [alla bolonyayzay]	with meat sauce
alla carbonara [alla karbonara]	with egg and bacon
alla marinara [alla mareenara]	with fish and seafood in tomato sauce
alla palermitana [alla palairmeetana]	with aubergines
Tortellini alla panna [tortelleenee alla panna]	tortellini in cream sauce

Pesci e frutti di mare

Calamari alla griglia [kalamaree alla greelya]	grilled squid
Calamari fritti [kalamaree freettee]	deep fried squid
Calamari al ragù [kalamaree al ragoo]	squid in tomato sauce
Cozze al vino bianco [kotzay al veeno byanko]	mussels in white wine
Grigliata mista di pesce [greelyata meesta dee payshay]	mixed grilled fish platter
Misto di frutti di mare [meesto dee froottee dee maray]	mixed seafood
Salmone alla pizzaiola [salmonay alla peetzayola]	salmon in tomato sauce with herbs
Scampi alla griglia [skampee alla greelya]	grilled king prawns
Sogliola alla griglia [solyola alla greelya]	grilled sole
Zuppa di pesce all'alloro [tsooppa dee payshay allalloro]	fish soup with bay leaf, tomatoes and herbs

Pizze

Calzone [kaltsonay]	folded pizza, stuffed with tomatoes, cheese, artichokes and ham
Capricciosa [kapreechoza]	with many different toppings
Margherita [margaireeta]	with tomato and mozzarella
Marinara [mareenara]	with tomatoes, cheese and seafood

Prosciutto [proshootto]	with tomatoes, cheese and cooked ham
Quattro stagioni [kwattro stajonee]	with tomatoes, cheese, sweet peppers, olives, ham and mushrooms
Romana [romana]	with anchovies
Salame [salamay]	with cheese and salami

Carni — Meat

Carne alla pizzaiola [karnay alla peetzayola]	beef in tomato sauce
Costata alla boscaiola [kostata alla boskayola]	loin with mushrooms in a cream sauce
Cotoletta alla bolognese [kotoletta alla bolonyayzay]	breaded escalope topped with cheese and ham
Cotoletta alla milanese [kotoletta alla meelanayzay]	escalope
Filetto alla griglia [feeletto alla greelya]	grilled fillet
Lombatina di maiale alla panna [lombateena dee mayalay alla panna]	pork loin in cream sauce
Ossobuco [ossobooko]	knuckle of veal
Rosbif [rosbeef]	beef stew
Saltimbocca alla Romana [salteembokka alla romana]	thinly cut loin with ham and sage in a wine sauce
Scaloppine al limone [skalopeenay al leemonay]	slices of veal in lemon sauce
Scaloppine al pepe [skalopeenay al paypay]	slices of veal in gorgonzola sauce with different types of pepper
Vitello trifolato [veetello treefolato]	finely chopped veal with mushrooms in a cream sauce

Selvaggina, pollame — Game, poultry

Anatra all'arancia [anatra allarancha]	duck with orange and ginger sauce
Cinghiale arrosto con carciofi e olive [cheengyalay arrosto kon karchofee ay oleevay]	wild boar with artichokes and olives
Fagiano arrosto con funghi misti [fajano arrosto kon foongee meestee]	roast pheasant with different types of mushrooms
Filetto di lepre in mantello di verza con funghi [feeletto dee lepray een mantello dee vairtsa kon foongee]	fillet of hare wrapped in savoy cabbage with mushrooms
Lombata di cervo con verdure primavera [lombata dee chairvo kon vairdooray preemavaira]	loin of venison served with a selection of vegetables
Pernice al vino bianco [pairneechay al veeno byanko]	partridge in white wine sauce
Pollo arrosto [pollo arrosto]	roast chicken
Quaglia alla cacciatora [kwalya alla kachatora]	quail served with tomato sauce, mushrooms and garlic

46

Contorni
Broccoli [**brok**koli]
Fagiolini [fajo**leenee**]
Finocchio [fee**nok**kyo]
Insalata di pomodori [insa**lata** di pomo**doree**]
Insalata mista [insa**lata mista**]
Insalata verde [insa**lata vair**day]
Patatine fritte [pata**teenay freet**tay]

Side dishes
broccoli
French beans
fennel
tomato salad
mixed salad
lettuce
chips

▶ **(Fruit and vegetables, see page 62)**

Formaggi
Asiago [a**zyago**]

Caciocavallo [kachoka**vallo**]

Gorgonzola [gorgond**zola**]
Mozzarella [motza**rella**]

Parmigiano [parmee**jano**]

Pecorino [peko**reeno**]
Provola [**provola**]
Ricotta [ree**kot**ta]

Cheese
hard cheese from the Asiago
area
ball-shaped cheese from
southern Italy
blue cheese
soft cheese made of buffalo
or cow's milk
hard cheese from the Parma
area
aromatic sheep cheese
smoked cheese
type of fromage frais

Dessert
Bignè all'amaretto [been**yay** allama**retto**]
Cannoli Siciliani [kan**nolee** seechee**lyanee**]
Cassata [ka**ssata**]
Coppa di melone [**kop**pa dee me**lonay**]
Favette [fa**vayt**tay]
Frutta di stagione [**froot**ta dee sta**jonay**]
Gelato [je**lato**]
Macedonia [mache**donya**]
Panna cotta [**panna kot**ta]
Tortine alla frutta [tor**teenay** alla **froot**ta]
Zabaione [tzaba**yonay**]

Desserts
Amaretto eclairs
Sicilian rolls
ice-cream with candied fruit
melon salad
deep fried pastry
seasonal fruit
ice-cream
fruit salad
cream dessert
fruit tartlets
marsala and egg cream

Gelati
Gelato al cioccolato
[je**lato** al choko**lato**]
Gelato al cocco [je**lato** al **kok**ko]
Gelato al mandarino
[je**lato** al manda**reeno**]
Gelato al pistacchio [je**lato** al pee**stak**yo]
Gelato alla banana [je**lato** alla ba**nana**]
Gelato alla vaniglia [je**lato** alla va**neel**ya]
Gelato alle castagne [je**lato** allay ka**stan**yay]
Gelato alle mandorle
[je**lato** allay **mandor**lay]
Meringhe ripiene di gelato
[me**reen**gay reep**yay**nay dee je**lato**]

Ice-cream
chocolate ice-cream

coconut ice-cream
tangerine ice-cream

pistachio ice-cream
banana ice-cream
vanilla ice-cream
chestnut ice-cream
almond ice-cream

meringue ice-cream

Sorbetti alla frutta [sorbettee alla frootta]	fruit sorbet
Sorbetto di albicocche [sorbetto dee albeekokay]	abricot sorbet
Sorbetto di ananas [sorbaytto dee ananas]	pineapple sorbet
Sorbetto di anguria [sorbetto dee angoorya]	melon sorbet
Sorbetto di fragole [sorbetto dee fragolay]	strawberry sorbet
Sorbetto di limoni [sorbetto dee leemonee]	lemon sorbet
Tartufo [tartoofo]	truffle ice-cream

Drinks

Bevande alcooliche	**Alcoholic drinks**
Acquavite [akwaveetay]	aquavite
Aperitivo [apaireeteevo]	apéritif
Cognac [konyak]	brandy
Birra [beerra]	beer
alla spina [alla speena]	draught
chiara/scura [kyara/skoora]	lager/brown ale
senza alcool [sendza alkool]	alcohol-free
Gin [jeen]	gin
Liquore [leekworay]	liqueur
Pònce [ponch]	punch
Rum [room]	rum
Sherri [shairree]	sherry
Spumante [spoomantay]	sparkling wine
Vermut [vairmoot]	vermouth
Vino [veeno]	wine
amabile/dolce [amabeelay/dolchay]	very sweet/sweet
bianco/rosso/rosato [byanko/rosso/rosato]	white/red/rosé
secco/mezzo secco [saykko/maytzo saykko]	dry/medium dry
Vino porto [veeno porto]	port
Whisky [veeskee]	whisky
con ghiaccio [kon gyacho]	on the rocks
soda [soda]	soda
Bevande rinfrescanti	**Soft drinks**
Acqua [akwa]	water
Acqua minerale [akwa meenairalay]	mineral water
gasata [gazata]	sparkling
naturale [natooralay]	still
Aranciata [aranchata]	orangeade
Frappé [frappay]	milk shake
Latte [lattay]	milk
Limonata [leemonata]	lemonade
Succo di arancia [sookko dee arancha]	orange juice
spremuta fresca [spremoota frayska]	freshly squeezed
Succo di frutta [sookko dee frootta]	fruit juice

▶ (Warm drinks, see breakfast, page 44)

Il Duomo, Milan's cathedral, towers over the city like a white marble mountain

Sightseeing

Tourist information

Is there/Are there
C'è [chay]

a tourist office
un ufficio di informazioni turistiche [oon oo**ffee**cho dee eenformats**yo**nay too**ree**steekay]

an information office
un ufficio informazioni [oon oo**ffee**cho eenformats**yo**nay

guided tours
una guida organizzata [**oo**na **gwee**da organee**tza**ta]

sightseeing tours of the city?
un giro della città? [oon **jee**ro **del**la **cheet**ta]

Do you have
Ha [a]

a street map
una carta topografica della città [**oo**na **kar**ta topo**gra**feeka **del**la **cheet**ta]

a map of the city centre/ the area
una carta del centro/dei dintorni [**oo**na **kar**ta del **chen**tro/**day**ee deen**tor**nee]

a map of the underground
un piano orario della metropolitana [oon pee**ay**ano o**ra**reeo **del**la metropoleetana]

brochures
prospetti [pros**pet**tee]

a list of hotels/ a list of restaurants
un elenco degli hotel/dei ristoranti [oon e**len**ko **day**lyee o**tel/day**ee reesto**ran**tee]

a programme of events
un programma delle manifestazioni [oon pro**gram**ma **del**lay maneefestats**yo**nay]

for this week/for the festival?
per questa settimana/ per le settimane festive? [pair **kwes**ta settee**ma**na/ pair lay settee**ma**nay fes**tee**vay]

Could you book a room for me?
Può riservarmi una camera? [pwo reesair**var**mee **oo**na ka**mai**ra]

Sightseeing

abbey	badia [badeea]
alley	vicolo [veekolo]
altar	altare [altaray]
ancient	antico [anteeko]
architecture	architettura [arkeetettoora]
arena	arena [arayna]
art	arte [artay]
artist	artista [arteesta]
arts and crafts	artigianato [arteejanato]
Baroque	barocco [barokko]
botanical gardens	giardino botanico [jardeeno botaneeko]
bridge	ponte [pontay]
building	edificio [edeefeecho]
castle	castello [kastello]
catacomb	catacombe [katakombay]
cave	caverna [kavairna]
ceiling fresco	affresco su soffitto [affresco soo soffeeto]
cemetery	cimitero [cheemeetairo]
century	secolo [saykolo]
chapel	cappella [kapella]
Christian	cristiano [kreestyano]
church service	messa [messa]
cloister	via crucis [veea kroochees]
cross	croce [krochay]
drawing	disegno [deesenyo]
emperor	imperatore [eempairatoray]
empress	imperatrice [eempairatreechay]
excavations	scavi [skavee]
facade	facciata [fachata]
fortress	fortezza [fortetza]
gallery	(galleria di) quadri [(gallaireea dee) kwadree]
garden	giardino [jardeeno]
gate	portone [portonay]
glass	vetro [vaytro]
gorge	burrone [boorronay]
Gothic	gotico [goteeko]
grotto	grotta [grotta]
guide	guida [gweeda]
history	storia [storya]
inscription	iscrizione [eeskreetsyonay]
island	isola [eezola]
king	re [ray]
lake	lago [lago]
landscape	paesaggio [pa-aysajjo]

library	biblioteca [beeblyotayka]
market	mercato [mairkato]
medieval	medioevale [medeeoevalay]
memorial	luogo commemorativo [lwogo kommemorateevo]
monastery	convento [konvento]
mosque	moschea [moskaya]
mountain	montagna [montanya]
national park	parco nazionale [parko natsyonalay]
nature reserve	zona protetta [dzona protetta]
old town	centro storico [chentro storeeko]
organ	organo [organo]
original	originale [oreejeenalay]
painting	pittura [peettoora]
panorama	panorama [panorama]
park	parco [parko]
pedestrian precinct	zona pedonale [dzona pedonalay]
picture	quadro [kwadro]
port	porto [porto]
prehistoric	preistorico [prayeestoreeko]
queen	regina [rayjeena]
relief	rilievo [reelyayvo]
religion	religione [releejonay]
renaissance	rinascimento [reenasheemento]
restore	restaurare [rest-owraray]
Romanesque	romanico [romaneeko]
roof	tetto [tetto]
ruin	rovina [roveena]
sculpture	scultura [skooltoora]
square	piazza [pyatza]
statue	statua [statooa]
temple	tempio [tempyo]
theatre	teatro [tayatro]
tomb	tomba [tomba]
tower	torre [torray]
town hall	municipio [mooneecheepyo]
town wall	mura della città [moora della cheetta]
traditions	usanze [oozantsay]
valley	valle [vallay]
view	vista [veesta]
vineyard	vigneto [veenyayto]
waterfall	cascata [kaskata]
wine tasting	assaggio di vino [assajjo dee veeno]
wood	bosco [bosko]
zoo	zoo [tzo]

What are the places of interest around here?

Cosa c'é di interessante da queste parti? [**koza** chay dee interes**san**tay da **kwes**tay **par**tee]

Visiting the sights

I'd like/We'd like to visit

Io vorrei/Noi vorremmo vedere
[ee-o vor**ray**ee/noy vor**ray**mmo ve**dair**ay]

the cathedral/the church
the palace/the castle

la cattedrale/la chiesa [la katay**dral**ay/la **kyay**za]
il palazzo/il castello. [eel pa**lat**zo/eel kas**tel**lo]

What are the opening hours of the exhibition/museum?

Quando è aperta la mostra/il museo? [**kwan**do ay a**pair**ta la **mos**tra/eel moo**zay**o]

Is there a guided tour in English?

C'è una guida (inglese)? [chay **oo**na **gwee**da (eenglay**zay**)]

When does it start?/How much is it?

Quando comincia?/Quanto costa? [**kwan**do ko**meen**cha/**kwan**to **kos**ta]

How long does it take?

Quanto dura? [**kwan**to **doo**ra]

1/2 ticket(s) for adults/children, please.

Un biglietto/Due biglietti, per adulti/bambini. [oon beel**yet**to/**doo**ay beel**yet**tee pair a**dool**tee/ bam**bee**nee]

Are there special rates for children/students/senior citizens?

C'è uno sconto per bambini/studenti/anziani? [chay **oo**no **skon**to pair bam**bee**nee/stoo**dayn**tee/ ant**sya**nee]

* Chiuso per rinnovo. [**kyoo**zo pair reen**no**vo]

Closed for renovation.

No cameras allowed!

Vietato fotografare! [vyay**ta**to fotogra**far**ay]

Do you have a guide in English?

Avete una guida in lingua inglese? [a**vay**tay **oo**na **gwee**da een **leen**gwa eenglay**zay**]

Excursions

How much is the excursion to ... ?

Quanto costa il viaggio per ...? [**kwan**to **kos**ta eel **vyaj**jo pair]

Do we have to pay extra for the meal/for admission charges?

Il vitto/I biglietti di entrata sono da pagare extra? [eel **veet**to/ee beel**yet**tee sono da pa**gar**ay **ay**xtra]

Two tickets for today's excursion/tomorrow's excursion/for the excursion at 10 o'clock to ..., please.

Prego due posti per la gita a ..., oggi/domani/ alle ore dieci. [**pray**go **doo**ay **pos**tee pair la **jee**ta a ..., **oj**jee/do**man**ee/**al**lay oray **dyay**chee]

When/Where do we meet?

Quando/Dov'è il posto di incontro? [**kwan**do/dovay eel **pos**to dee een**kon**tro]

When do we get back?

Quando ritorniamo? [**kwan**do reetorn**yam**o]

Do we have

Abbiamo [abb**yam**o]

time to go shopping?
time to ourselves?

tempo per le spese [**tem**po pair lay **spay**zay]
tempo libero a disposizione?
[**tem**po **lee**bairo a deesposeets**yon**ay]

Do we also visit ...?

Visitiamo anche ...? [veezeet**yam**o an**kay**]

Taking it easy on one of Italy's many fine beaches

Active Pursuits

At the beach and at the swimming pool

Is there ... around here?
an open air/indoor
swimming pool
a place to hire boats?

C'è ... qui vicino? [chay kwee veecheeno]
una piscina libera/coperta
[**oo**na pee**shee**na **lee**baira/ko**pair**ta]
un'affittabarche [oonaffeetta**bar**kay]

Is there a strong current?

La corrente è pericolosa?
[la ko**rren**tay ay paireeko**lo**za]

Are there jellyfish/sea urchins
in the water?

Ci sono meduse/ricci in acqua?
[chee **so**no me**doo**zay/**ree**chee een **ak**wa]

I'd like/We'd like to hire

Io vorrei/Noi vorremmo affittare
[**ee**-o vo**rray**ee/noy vo**rray**mo affeet**ta**ray]

a (pedal/motor/
rowing/sailing) boat
a deckchair
a surfboard
a pair of water skis.

una barca (a pedale/motore/remi/vela)
[**oo**na **bar**ka (a pe**da**lay/mo**to**ray/**ray**mee/**vay**la)]
una sedia a sdraio [**oo**na **say**dya a **zdra**yo]
una tavola da surf [**oo**na **ta**vola da surf]
sci da acqua. [shee da **ak**wa]

How much is it
per half hour
per day
per week?

Quanto costa [**kwan**to **kos**ta]
per mezzora [pair met**zo**ra]
al giorno [al **jor**no]
per una settimana? [pair **oo**na settee**ma**na]

Are there ... around here?
sailing courses/schools
surfing courses/schools

Ci sono [chee **so**no]
corsi/scuole per vela [**kor**see/**skwo**lay pair **vay**la]
corsi/scuole per surf? [**kor**see/**skwo**lay pair surf]

I'm a beginner/
I'm experienced.

Io sono principiante/pratico.
[**ee**-o **so**no preencheepy**an**tay/**pra**teeko]

Danger signs

Avviso di tempesta	Storm warning!
Pericoloso	Danger
Solo per nuotatori	Swimmers only!
Vietato fare il bagno	No swimming!
Vietato tuffarsi	No jumping!

Sports

Is there ... around here?
C'è/Ci sono [chay/chee sono]

a place to hire bikes
biciclette da affittare
[beecheeklettay da affeettaray]

a (crazy) golf course
un campo per (mini)golf
[oon kampo pair (mini)golf]

a tennis court
un campo da tennis? [oon kampo da tennis]

Where can I
Dov'è possibile
[dovay posseebeelay]

go bowling/
go horse riding
giocare a birilli/cavalcare
[jokaray a beereellee/kavalkaray]

play squash/table
tennis/tennis?
giocare a squash/ping-pong/tennis? [jokaray a squash/pingpong/tennis]

Is fishing/swimming allowed here?
Si può pescare/fare il bagno qui?
[see pwo peskaray/faray eel banyo kwee]

I'd like/We'd like to hire
Io vorrei/Noi vorremmo affittare
[ee-o vorrayee/noy vorraymo affeettaray]

cross-country skis/downhill skis
sci da fondo/sci da discesa
[shee da fondo/shee da deeshayza]

ice skating boots
pattini [patteenee]

a tennis racket.
una racchetta da tennis.
[oona raketta da tennis]

Do you play chess?
Giochi/Gioca a scacchi? [jokkee/jokka a skakkee]

Do you mind if I join in?
Posso giocare anche io?
[posso jokkaray ankay ee-o]

Nature, environment, adventure

We'd like
Noi vorremo [noy vorraymo]

to go on a bicycle tour
fare un'escursione con la bicicletta
[faray ooneskoorsyonay kon la beecheekletta]

to go hiking
fare un giro in montagna
[faray oon jeero een montanya]

to go trekking
fare un'escursione [faray ooneskoorsyonay]

in the nature reserve
attraverso il territorio protetto
[attravairso eel tairreetoryo protetto]

in the national park.
attraverso il parco nazionale.
[attravairso eel parko natsyonalay]

Do you have
a hiking map?

Ha [a]
una mappa per escursioni?
[**oo**na **ma**ppa pair eskoor**syo**nee]

Is the route
easy/difficult
well marked
suitable for children?

La gita è [la **jee**ta ay]
semplice/difficile [**sem**pleechay/dee**ffee**cheelay]
ben segnata [ben sen**ya**ta]
adatta per bambini? [a**dat**ta pair bam**bee**nee]

How long will it take?

Quanto dura la gita?
[**kwan**to **doo**ra la **jee**ta]

Is this the right way
to …?

È questa la strada giusta per …?
[ay **kwes**ta la **stra**da **joos**ta pair]

Active pursuits

aerobics	aerobica [a-ai**ro**beeka]
arm bands	braccioli [bra**cho**lee]
badminton	volano [**vo**lano]
ball	palla [**pal**la]
basketball	palla da basket [**pal**la da **bas**ket]
bay	baia [**ba**ya]
billiards	bigliardo [beel**yar**do]
changing rooms	cabina [ka**bee**na]
danger of avalanches	pericolo di valanghe [pai**ree**kolo dee va**lan**gay]
diving equipment	attrezzatura da sommozzatore [attretza**too**ra da sommotza**to**ray]
flippers	pinne [**peen**nay]
gymnastics	ginnastica [jeen**nas**teeka]
health club	centro sportivo [**chen**tro spor**tee**vo]
horse	cavallo [ka**val**lo]
jogging	jogging [**jog**ging]
net	pallacanestro [pallaka**nes**tro]
playground	campo da gioco [**kam**po da **jok**ko]
pony	pony [**po**nee]
ride	passeggiata a cavallo [passay**ja**ta a ka**val**lo]
rubber dinghy	gommone [gom**mo**nay]
sauna	sauna [**sao**na]
shade	ombra [**om**bra]
shells	conchiglie [kon**keel**yay]
shower	doccia [**do**cha]
skating	pattinare sul ghiaccio [patte**na**ray sool **gya**cho]
sled	slitta [**zleet**ta]
snorkelling	immergersi con il respiratore [eemair**jair**see kon eel respeera**to**ray]
snow	neve [**nay**vay]
stadium	stadio [**stad**yo]
storm	tempesta [tem**pes**ta]
suntan lotion	crema da sole [**kray**ma da **so**lay]
volleyball	palla a volo [**pal**la a **vo**lo]
wave	onda [**on**da]

ACTIVE PURSUITS

How far is it to ...?   Quanto è ancora lontano fino a ...?
                                 [**kwan**to ay an**kor**a lontano **fee**no a]

Courses

I'd like to attend   **Io vorrei iscrivermi a**
                                 [ee-o vor**ray**ee ees**kree**vairmee a]
a language course   un corso di lingua [oon **kor**so dee **leen**gwa]
a cookery/painting course   un corso di cucina/di pittura
                                 [oon **kor**so dee koo**chee**na/dee peet**toor**a]
a dance workshop.   un corso di ballo. [oon **kor**so dee **bal**lo]

Are there still places   Ci sono ancora posti liberi?
available?   [chee **so**no an**kor**a **pos**tee **lee**bairee]
Where does the course/   Dove si fa il corso/il seminario?
the seminar take place?   [**do**vay see fa eel **kor**so/eel semee**nar**yo]
How many people are taking   Quanti partecipanti ha il corso?
part in the course?   [**kwan**tee partechee**pan**tee a eel **kor**so]
When does it start?/How   Quando comincia/Quanto costa il corso?
much is the course?   [**kwan**do ko**meen**cha/**kwan**to **kos**ta eel **kor**so]
Do you have somebody to   C'è un'assistenza per bambini?
look after the children?   [chay oonassee**sten**tsa pair bam**bee**nee]
I have (good) previous   Io ho (buone) conoscenze di base.
knowledge   [ee-o o (bwonay) kono**shen**zay dee **ba**zay]
I don't have any previous   Io non ho conoscenze di base.
knowledge   [ee-o non o kono**shen**zay dee **ba**zay]

The oldest sports newspaper in the world

In Italy sport is not just another topic of conversation. For many Italians it is the only thing that matters. This obsession is exemplified by the oldest newspaper in the world to deal exclusively in sport, *La Gazzetta dello Sport*. On 3 April 1996 the pink sporting gazette celebrated its 100th birthday. It is a national institution which sells about 350,000 copies a day and yet still looks young and fresh. The editor-in-chief, Candido Cannovò, believes he runs more than just a newspaper. He says it actually provides an emotional focus for an entire nation. On a Monday morning after a weekend of sporting events, the *Gazzetta dello Sport* is the most-read and most-discussed daily newspaper in the country. Football fans wanting to read about the burning issues in Italy's footballing world may need to know the relevant terminology:

defeat sconfitta [skon**feet**ta]
defender difensore [deefen**sor**ay]
draw pareggio [pa**ray**djo]
first/second half primo/secondo tempo [**preemo**/se**kon**do **tem**po]
football fan tifoso [tee**fozo**]
forward attaccante [atta**kan**tay]
foul fallo [**fal**lo]
goal goal [gol]
goalkeeper portiere [port**yair**ay]
off fuori [**fwor**ee]
off-side fuori di campo [**fwor**ee dee **kam**po]
penalty calcio di rigore [**kal**cho dee ree**gor**ay]
player giocatore [jokka**tor**ay]
referee arbitro [**arbeet**ro]
result risultato [reezool**tat**o]
team squadra [**skwad**ra]
top goalscorer capocannoniere [kapokannon**yair**ay]
victory vittoria [veet**tor**eea]

Traditional masks at the Venice carnival

Entertainment

Cinema, theatre, opera and concerts

Whats on at the cinema today/tomorrow?	Quali film danno oggi/domani al cinema? [**kwa**lee film **dan**no **oj**jee/doma**nee** al **chee**nayma]
Is the film	**Il film è** [eel film ay]
dubbed	sincronizzato [seenkronee**tza**to]
shown in the original version with subtitles?	in versione originale con sottotitoli? [een vairs**yo**nay oreejee**na**lay kon sotto**tee**tolee]
When does . . . start?	**Quando comincia** [**kwan**do ko**meen**cha]
the show	la presentazione [la presentats**yo**nay]
the film	il film principale [eel film preen**chee**palay]
the concert	il concerto [eel kon**chair**to]
the matinée	la matinée [la matte**e**nay]
the ballet performance	la rappresentazione del balletto [la rappresentats**yo**nay del bal**lc**tto]
the cabaret	il cabaret [eel kaba**ret**]
the opera	l'opera [**lo**paira]
the operetta	l'operetta [lopai**ret**ta]
the musical	il musical [eel **moo**zeekal]
the play	la rappresentazione [la raprezentats**yo**nay]
the ticket sale	la vendita anticipata dei biglietti [la **ven**deeta anteechee**pa**ta **day**ee beel**yet**tee]
for the festival ?	per il festival? [pair eel **fes**teeval]

At the theatre

Centro centre	**Loggia** box
Destra/Sinistra right/left	**Platea** stalls
Fila row	**Posto** seat
Gabinetti toilets	**Prima/Seconda categoria**
Galleria gallery	dress/upper circle
Lato aisle	**Uscita di emergenza** emergency exit

What's on

tonight/tomorrow night
this weekend

at the theatre/at the opera

Is there a concert on (this evening)?

Where do I get/How much are tickets?

Are there still tickets at the box office?

Are there special rates?

* Tutto venduto.
[**too**tto ven**doo**to]

Two tickets/seats . . ., please.

for the show

for the concert
tonight/tomorrow night
at 8 o'clock

How long does the show last?

I would like a programme, please.

Che cosa si dà
[kay **ko**za see da]
oggi/domani sera [**oj**jee/do**ma**nee **sai**ra]
questo fine settimana
[**kwes**to **fee**nay set**tee**mana]
a teatro/all'opera [a ta**ya**tro/allo**pai**ra]

C'è un concerto stasera [chay oon con**chai**rto (sta**sai**ra)?]

Dove si ricevono/Quanto costano i biglietti?
[**do**vay see ree**chay**vono/**kwan**to **kos**tano ee beel**yet**tee]

Ci sono ancora biglietti alla cassa?
[chee **so**no an**ko**ra beel**yet**tee alla **kas**sa]

Ci sono biglietti ridotti?
[chee **so**no beel**yet**tee ree**dot**tee]

Sold out.

Prego due biglietti/posti
[**pray**go **doo**ay beel**yet**tee/**pos**tee]
per la rappresentazione
[pair la rappresentats**yo**nay]
per il concerto [pair eel kon**chai**rto]
oggi/domani sera [**oj**jee/do**ma**nee **sai**ra]
alle ore venti. [**al**lay **o**ray **ven**tee]

Quanto dura la rappresentazione?
[**kwan**to **doo**ra la rappresentats**yo**nay]

Io vorrei un programma.
[**ee**-o vor**ray**ee oon pro**gram**ma]

Nightlife

Is there . . . around here?
a discotheque
a (nice) pub
a bar
a casino
with live music?

C'è . . . da queste parti [chay da **kwes**tay **par**tee]
una discoteca [**oo**na deesko**tay**ka]
una cantina (carina) [**oo**na kan**tee**na (ka**ree**na)]
un bar [oon bar]
un casinò [oon kazee**no**]
con musica (live)? [kon **moo**zeeka (live)]

Is this seat taken?	È ancora libero qui? [ay an**kora lee**bairo kwee]
Could I see the wine list, please.	La carta delle bevande, prego. [la **kar**ta **del**lay be**van**day **pray**go]

Shall we
  dance
  have a drink
  get a bit of fresh air?

Vorrebbe [vor**reb**bay]
  ballare [bal**la**ray]
  bere qualcosa [**bair**ay kwal**ko**za]
  prendere aria fresca? [**pren**dairay **ar**ya **fres**ka]

This one's on me.	Io la invito. [**ee**-o la een**vee**to]

Entertainment

actor	attore [at**to**ray]
actress	attrice [at**tree**chay]
band	banda [**ban**da]
bar	bar [bar]
bouncer	usciere [oosh**yai**ray]
box office	cassa [**kas**sa]
cabaret	cabaret [kaba**ret**]
chamber music	musica da camera [**moo**zeeka da **kam**aira]
choir	coro [**ko**ro]
circus	circo [**cheer**ko]
comedy	commedia [kom**med**eea]
concert	concerto [kon**chair**to]
conductor	direttore [deeret**to**ray]
dance hall	locale da ballo [lo**ka**lay da **bal**lo]
dancer	ballerino/ballerina [ballai**ree**no/ballai**ree**na]
director	regista [ray**jee**sta]
folk concert	serata folcloristica [sai**ra**ta folklo**rees**teeka]
go out	uscire [oo**shee**ray]
interval	pausa [**pow**za]
jazz concert	concerto jazz [kon**chair**to jazz]
open-air theatre	teatro all'aperto [tay**a**tro alla**pair**to]
opera glasses	binocolo [bee**nok**kolo]
orchestra	orchestra [or**kes**tra]
play (vb)	suonare [swo**na**ray]
play (noun)	rappresentazione [rapprezentats**yo**nay]
pop music	musica pop [**moo**zeeka pop]
première	prima [**pree**ma]
presentation	rappresentazione [rapresentats**yo**nay]
singer	cantante [kan**tan**tay]
stage	palcoscenico [palko**shen**eeko]
stage set	scenario [shen**ar**yo]
ticket	biglietto di entrata [beel**yet**to dee en**tra**ta]

Can I	**Posso accompagnarti/accompagnarla**
	[**pos**so akompan**yar**ti/akompan**yar**la]
walk a bit with you	un pezzo [oon **pet**zo]
walk you home	a casa [a **ka**za]
walk you to the hotel?	in albergo/hotel?
	[een al**bair**go/o**tel**]
Would you like to come to my place?	Vorresti/Vorrebbe venire ancora da me?
	[vor**res**tee/vor**reb**bay ve**nee**ray an**ko**ra da may]
Thank you very much for the nice evening.	Grazie per questa bella serata.
	[**grats**yay pair **kwes**ta **bel**la sai**ra**ta]
Good-bye./ See you tomorrow!	Arrivederci./A domani.
	[arreevay**dair**chee/a do**ma**nee]

Festivals and events

When does ... start?	**Quando comincia**
	[**kwan**do ko**meen**cha]
the festival	la festa (popolare)
	[la **fes**ta (popo**la**ray)]
the festival programme	il programma festivo
	[eel pro**gram**ma fes**tee**vo]
the (trade) fair	la fiera [la fee**ai**ra]
the matinée	la matinée [la mate**e**nay]
the parade/procession	il corteo/la processione
	[eel kor**tay**o/la proches**syo**nay]
the show/performance	lo show/la rappresentazione
	[lo show/la raprezentats**yo**nay]
the circus?	la presentazione del circo?
	[la presentats**yo**nay del **cheer**ko]
Where does the show take place?	Dove si dà la manifestazione?
	[**do**vay see da la maneefestayts**yo**nay]
How long will it last?	Quanto durerà?
	[**kwan**to doo**rai**ra]
Do you have to pay to get in?	Si deve pagare l'entrata?
	[see **day**vay pa**ga**ray len**tra**ta]
Where do I get/ How much are the tickets?	Dove ricevo/Quanto costano i biglietti?
	[**do**vay ree**chay**vo/**kwan**to **kos**tano ee beel**yet**tee]

La Passeggiata

During the warm summer evenings and Sunday afternoons, Italians love to take a stroll. After 4pm, when the shops re-open, people pour on to the shopping streets, squares and into the bars. After work friends and families gather for their *cena fuori*, a meal in a restaurant. The early evening stroll, known as *la passeggiata*, is the opportunity to meet, chat and to see and be seen. The piazza and side streets become a parade ground for young men and women to show off their new clothes and flirt. Despite the distractions of television, *la passeggiata* is for many people still an essential everyday ritual.

The markets are still the main shopping centres for both locals and tourists alike

Shopping

General

Where can I get

films
papers?

Dove ci sono/Dove posso trovare
[**do**vay chee **so**no/**do**vay **pos**so trova**ra**y]
pellicole [pel**lee**kolay]
giornali? [jor**na**lee]

Is there ... around here?
a bakery
a food store

a butcher's shop
a supermarket

C'è ... qui vicino? [chay kwee vee**chee**no]
una panetteria [**oo**na panettai**ree**a]
un negozio di generi alimentari
[oon ne**gots**yo dee **jay**nairee aleemen**ta**ree]
una macelleria [**oo**na machellai**ree**a)
un supermercato [oon soopairmair**ka**to]

* **Cosa desidera?**
[**ko**sa de**see**daira]
* **Posso aiutarla?**
[**po**sso ayoo**tar**la]

What would you like?

Can I help you?

I'm just looking, thanks.

Io vorrei solo dare un'occhiata.
[**ee**-o vor**ra**yee solo **da**ray oonok**ya**ta]

I'd like ..., please.
stamps
suntan lotion

Per favore vorrei [pair fa**vo**ray vor**ra**yee]
francobolli [franko**bol**lee]
una crema da sole. [**oo**na **kray**ma da **so**lay]

How much is this?
That's (too) expensive.

Quanto costa? [**kwan**to **kos**ta]
È (troppo) caro. [ay (**trop**po) **ka**ro]

I (don't) like that.

I'll take it.

Questo (non) mi piace.
[**kwes**to (non) mee pya**chay**]
Lo prendo. [lo **pren**do]

61

Groceries

baby food	alimenti per neonati [aleementee pair nayonatee]
biscuits	biscotti [beeskottee]
butter	burro [boorro]
cake	dolce [dolchay]
chocolate	cioccolata [chokkolata]
(without) colouring	(senza) coloranti [(sendza) kolorantee]
cream	panna [panna]
eggs	uova [wova]
fish	pesce [payshay]
flour	farina [fareena]
fruit	frutta [frootta]
juice	succo [sooko]
ketchup	ketchup [ketchup]
margarine	margarina [margareena]
mayonnaise	maionese [mayonayzay]
meat	carne [karnay]
(full-cream/semi-skimmed)	latte (intero/scremato)
milk	[lattay (eentairo/skremato)]
mortadella	mortadella [mortadella]
mustard	senape [saynapay]
nuts	noci [nochee]
oil	olio [olyo]
paprika	peperone [pepaironay]
pepper	pepe [paypay]
porridge oats	fiocchi di avena [fyokkee dee avayna]
(without) preservatives	(senza) conservanti [(sendza) konsairvantee]
rusk	fette biscottate [fettay beeskottatay]
salt	sale [salay]
spices	spezie [spetsyay]
sugar	zucchero [tsukkairo]
tinned foods	conserve [konsairvay]
toast	toast [tost]
vegetable	verdura [vairdoora]
vinegar	aceto [achayto]

▶ (See also food, page 44)

Fruit and vegetables

apple	mela [mayla]
apricot	albicocca [albeekokka]
artichoke	carciofo [karchofo]
aubergine	melanzana [melantsana]

avocado	avocado [avo**ka**do]
banana	banana [ba**na**na]
basil	basilico [ba**zee**leeko]
beans	fagioli [fa**jo**lee]
broccoli	broccoli [**brok**kolee]
cabbage	cavolo [**ka**volo]
carrots	carote [ka**rot**tay]
cherries	ciliegie [cheel**yay**jay]
chick peas	ceci [**chay**chee]
chicory	cicoria [chee**kor**ya]
chilli	peperoncini [pepairon**chee**nee]
courgettes	zucchini [tsoo**kee**nee]
cucumber	cetriolo [chetree**o**lo]
dates	datteri [**dat**tairee]
fennel	finocchio [fee**nok**kyo]
figs	fichi [**fee**kee]
garlic	aglio [**al**yo]
grapes (white/red)	uva (bianca/nera) [**oo**va (by**an**ka/**nai**ra)]
kiwi	kiwi [**kee**wee]
leeks	porro [**por**ro]
lemon	limone [lee**mo**nay]
mandarin orange	mandarino [manda**ree**no]
mango	mango [**man**go]
melon	melone [me**lo**nay]
nectarine	mandarino dolce [manda**ree**no **dol**chay]
olives	olive [o**lee**vay]
onion	cipolla [chee**pol**la]
orange	arancia [a**ran**cha]
parsley	prezzemolo [pret**zay**molo]
peanuts	arachidi [ara**kee**dee]
pear	pera [**pai**ra]
peas	piselli [pee**zel**lee]
pineapple	ananas [**a**nanas]
plum	prugna [**proon**ya]
potatoes	patate [pa**ta**tay]
raspberries	lamponi [lam**po**nee]
runner beans	fagiolini [fajo**lee**nee]
sweetcorn	granoturco [grano**toor**ko]
sweet pepper	peperone [pepai**ro**nay]
spinach	spinaci [spee**na**chee]
tomato	pomodoro [pomo**do**ro]
watermelon	anguria [an**goor**ya]

The market

The market *(mercato)* is still the place Italians prefer to get their shopping – much more so than the supermarket. Towns and villages have a market day at least once a week. Every market has its own special character and local specialities. As well as food, there are usually stalls selling clothes, household goods, farming and DIY tools, livestock and much more, depending on the size of the market.

The range of goods on offer is often wider and more varied than you'll find in a department store or a supermarket. It is not unusual to see customers haggling with traders over prices.

Do you have anything else cheaper/larger/smaller?

Ha qualcos'altro di più economico/più grande/ più piccolo? [a kwalko**zal**tro dee pyoo eko**no**meeko/pyoo **gran**day/pyoo **peek**kolo]

Can I
 pay by cheque/ traveller's cheque/credit card

 exchange this?

Posso [**pos**so]
 pagare con assegno/traveller's cheque/ carta di credito [**pos**so pa**ga**ray kon as**sen**yo/ travellers**sheks**/**kar**ta dee **kre**deeto]
 cambiare questo? [kamb**ya**ray **kwes**to]

Where's the nearest cash dispenser/ the nearest bank?

Dov'è il prossimo bancomat/la prossima banca? [do**vay** eel **pros**seemo **ban**komat/la **pros**seema **ban**ka]

* Ancora qualcosa? [an**ko**ra kwal**ko**za]

Anything else?

That's all, thanks.
Could you pack it for me, please?
Do you have a carrier bag?

Grazie è tutto. [**grats**yay ay **toot**to]
Mi può fare un pacchetto?
[mee pwo **fa**ray oon pak**ket**to]
Posso avere una busta? [**pos**so a**vai**ray **oo**na **boos**ta]

Groceries

I'd like/Could I have ...,
please?
 a piece of ...
 100 grams of...
 half a kilo of ...
 a kilo of ...
 a litre of ...
 a tin of ...
 a bottle of ...

Vorrei/Mi dia per favore
[vor**ray**ee/mee **dee**a pair fa**vo**ray]
 un pezzo di ... [oon **pet**zo dee]
 cento grammi di ... [**chen**to **gram**mee dee]
 mezzo chilo di ... [**met**zo **kee**lo dee]
 un chilo di ... [oon **kee**lo dee]
 un litro di ... [oon **lee**tro dee]
 una lattina di ... [**oo**na lat**tee**na dee]
 una bottiglia di ... [**oo**na bot**tee**lya dee]

Could I try some please?

Ne posso assaggiare? [nay **pos**so assa**ja**ray]

* Va bene un po' in più? [va **bay**nay oon po een pyoo]

It's a bit over. Is that all right?

A bit more/less, please.

Un po di più/di meno prego. [oon po dee pyoo/dee **may**no **pray**go]

It's all right!

Lasci così! [**la**shee ko**zee**]

Books, stationery and newspapers

Do you sell	**Ha** [a]
English papers/magazines	giornali/riviste in inglese
	[**jor**nalee/ree**vees**tay een een**glay**zay]
postcards	cartoline illustrate [kar**to**leenay eelloo**stra**tay]
stamps	francobolli [franko**bol**lee]
envelopes	buste per lettera [**boos**tay pair **let**taira]
pens/pencils	penne a biro/matite [**pen**nay a **bee**ro/ma**tee**tay]
English books	libri in inglese [**lee**bree een een**glay**zay]
glue/adhesive tape?	colla/nastro adesivo? [**kol**la/**nas**tro ada**yzee**vo]

I'd like	**Io vorrei** [ee-o vor**ray**ee]
a map of ...	una carta geografica di ...
	[**oo**na **kar**ta jayogra**fee**ka dee]
a street map	una carta della città [**oo**na **kar**ta **del**la **cheet**ta]
a travel guide	una guida turistica [**oo**na **gwee**da too**ree**steeka]
an Italian–English	un dizionario italiano-inglese.
dictionary.	[oon deetseeo**na**reeo eeta**lya**no-een**glay**zay]

Clothes and shoes

I'm looking for	**Io cerco** [**ee**o **chair**ko]
a blouse/a shirt	una camicetta/una camicia
	[**oo**na kamee**chet**ta/**oo**na ka**mee**cha]
a T-shirt	una maglietta [**oo**na mal**yet**ta]
a pair of trousers/a skirt/	dei pantaloni/una gonna/un vestito
a dress	[**day**ee panta**lo**nee/**oo**na **gon**na/oon ves**tee**to]
a sweater/a jacket	un maglione/una giacca
	[oon mal**yo**nay/**oo**na **jak**ka]
underwear/socks	biancheria intima/calzini
	[byankai**ree**a een**tee**ma/kalt**see**nee]
a raincoat	una giacca impermeabile
	[**oo**na **jak**ka eempairmaya**bee**lay]
a pair of shoes.	scarpe. [**skar**pay]

I take size 40/I take size 39.	Io ho la taglia quaranta/il numero di scarpe trentanove. [ee-o o la **tal**ya kwa**ran**ta/eel **noo**mairo dee **skar**pay trenta**no**vay]
Could I try this on?	Posso provare? [**pos**so pro**var**ay]
Do you have a mirror?	Dov'è uno specchio? [do**vay oo**no **spek**yo]
It fits/doesn't fit nicely.	Questo (non) mi sta bene. [**kwes**to (non) mee sta **bay**nay]
I like/I don't like it/this colour.	Questo/Questo colore (non) mi piace. [**kwes**to/**kwes**to ko**lor**ay (non) mee **pya**chay]
I'll take it.	Io lo prendo. [ee-o lo **pren**do]
Do you have other models/colours?	Ci sono ancora altri modelli/colori? [chee **so**no an**kor**a **al**tree mo**del**lee/ko**lor**ee]

It is	**È** [ay]
too small/big	troppo piccolo/grande [**trop**po **peek**olo/**gran**day]
too long/short	troppo lungo/corto [**trop**po **loon**go/**kor**to]

Is this	**Questo/Questa è** [**kwes**to/**kwes**ta ay]
real leather	vera pelle [**vair**a **pel**lay]
cotton/wool/silk/linen?	cotone/lana/seta/lino? [ko**ton**ay/**lan**a/**say**ta/**leen**o]

Laundry and dry cleaning

I'd like to have these things cleaned/washed.	Io vorrei fare pulire/lavare questo. [ee-o vor**ray**ee **far**ay poo**leer**ay/la**var**ay **kwes**to]
How much is it?	Quanto costa? [**kwan**to **kos**ta]
When can I pick it up?	Quando posso venire a prenderlo? [**kwan**do **pos**so ve**neer**ay a **pren**dairlo]

Jewellery and watches

My necklace/my alarm clock is broken.	La mia catenina/La mia sveglia è rotta. [la **mee**-a katay**neen**a/la **mee**-a **svel**ya ay **rot**ta]
My watch is broken.	Il mio orologio è rotto. [eel **mee**-o oro**lo**jo ay **rot**to]
Could you repair it?	Può riparare questo/-a? [pwo reepa**rar**ay **kwes**to/-a]

I'd like	**Io avrei bisogno di** [ee-o av**ray** beez**on**yo dee]
a new battery	una nuova batteria [**oo**na **nwo**va battai**ree**a]
a bracelet	un bracciale [oon bra**chal**ay]
a brooch	una spilla [**oo**na **speel**la]
a ring	un anello [oon a**nel**lo]
some earrings.	orecchini. [orek**keen**ee]

Buying clothes in Italy

When buying clothes and shoes in Italy, you'll find that the Italian sizing system is different to the British. With women's clothing, add 32 to your UK size, so a woman's 12, for example, becomes 44. The difference in men's shirt sizes is 23, so a size 16 collar becomes a 39. With suits simply add 10 (UK40 is 50 in Italy). Shoe sizes are different too. Add 33 to your UK size (UK6 = 39).

Clothes and shoes

anorak	anorak [anorak]
belt	cintura [cheentoora]
bikini	bikini [beekeenee]
boots	stivali [steevalee]
bra	reggiseno [rejeesayno]
cap	berretto [bairetto]
gloves	guanti [gwantee]
hat	cappello [kappello]
panties	slip [zleep]
sandals	sandali [sandalee]
scarf	foulard [foolar]
sunhat	cappello da sole [kappello da solay]
swimming trunks	slip da bagno [zleep da banyo]
swimsuit	costume da bagno [kostoomay da banyo]
tie	cravatta [kravatta]
tights	collant [kollan]
tracksuit	tuta da ginnastica [toota da jeennasteeka]
waistcoat	gilet [jeelay]

Is this	È/Sono [ay/sono]
genuine	vero/veri [vairo/vairee]
silver/gold	d'argento/d'oro [darjento/doro]
silver-plated/gold-plated?	argentato/dorato? [arjentato/dorato]

Electrical appliances and photography

I'm looking for/I need	Io cerco/Ho bisogno di [ee-o chairko/o beezonyo dee]
an adapter	una spina di riduzione [oona speena dee reedootsyonay]
a battery	una batteria [oona battaireea]
for a torch	per torcia elettrica [pair torcha elettreeka]
for a camera	per macchina fotografica [pair makkeena fotografeeka]
for a video camera	per videocamera [pair veedeokamaira]
for a radio.	per radio. [pair radyo]

I'd like	Io avrei bisogno di [ee-o avrayee beezonyo dee]
a colour film/a black and white film	una pellicola a colori/bianco e nero [oona pelleekola a koloree/byanko ay nairo]
a slide film	una pellicola per diapositiva [oona pelleekola pair deeapozeeteeva]
with 24/36 exposures	per ventiquattro/trentasei riprese [pair venteekwattro/trentasayee reeprayzay]
a video casette (VHS)	una cassetta video (VHS) [oona kassetta veedeo (voo-akka essay)]
a standard lens	un obiettivo standard [oon obyetteevo standard]
a wide-angle/ telephoto/zoom lens.	un obiettivo grandangolare/tele/zoom. [oon obyetteevo grandangolaray/taylay/tzoom]

Could you ..., please?
  put the film in the camera
  develop this film for me

  do prints
    9 by 13

  gloss/matt

Può/Potete [pwo/potaytay]
  mettere la pellicola [**met**tairay la pel**lee**kola]
  sviluppare questa pellicola
  [sveeloo**par**ay **kwes**ta pel**lee**kola]
  sviluppare delle foto [sveeloo**par**ay **del**lay **fo**to]
    in formato nove per tredici
    [een for**ma**to **no**vay pair **tray**deechee]
  lucido/opaco? [**loo**cheedo/o**pa**kko]

Do you do passport photos?
When will the prints be
ready?

Lei fa foto per tessera? [lay fa **fo**to pair **tes**saira]
Quando sono pronte le foto?
[**kwan**do sono **pron**tay lay **fo**to]

... doesn't work.
  My camera

  My flash

... non funziona bene. [non foontsy**o**na **bay**nay]
  La mia macchina fotografica
  [la **mee**-a **mak**keena foto**gra**feeka]
  Il mio flash [eel **mee** o flash]

Could you have a look at
it?/Can you repair it?

Può controllarlo/-la/ripararlo/-la?
[pwo kontrol**lar**lo/la/reepa**rar**lo/la]

When can I pick it up?

Quando posso venire a prenderlo/prenderli?
[**kwan**do **pos**so ve**nee**ray a **pren**dairlo/**pren**dairlee]

Souvenirs and arts and crafts

I'm looking for
  a souvenir
  folk costumes
  ceramics
  art
    modern/antique/folk

  leather goods
  jewellery.

Io cerco [ee-o **chair**ko]
  un souvenir [oon soove**neer**]
  vestiti folcloristici [ves**tee**tee folklo**ree**steechee]
  ceramica [chai**ra**meeka]
  oggetti artistici [o**jet**tee ar**tees**steechee]
    moderni/antichi/popolari
    [mo**dair**nee/an**tee**kee/**pop**polaree]
  oggetti in pelle [o**jet**tee een **pel**lay]
  gioielli. [jo**yel**lee]

What's typical of
  this town
  this area
  this country?

Cosa è tipico per [**ko**za ay tee**pee**ko pair]
  questa città [**kwes**ta chee**tta**]
  questa regione [**kwes**ta re**jo**nay]
  questo paese? [**kwes**to pa-**ay**zay]

Is this
  handmade
  genuine/antique
  artisan work
  local?

Questo è [**kwes**to ay]
  fatto a mano [**fat**to a **ma**no]
  vero/antico [**vai**ro/an**tee**ko]
  artigianato artistico [artee**ja**nato ar**tees**teeko]
  della regione? [**del**la re**jo**nay]

Optician

My glasses are broken.

I miei occhiali sono rotti.
[ee my**ay**ee ok**kya**lee sono **rot**tee]

Can you let me have a
substitute pair?

Può darmi degli occhiali di riserva?
[pwo **dar**mee **day**lyee ok**kya**lee dee ree**sair**va]

Chemist

baby powder	talco per bambini [**tal**ko pair bam**bee**nee]
baby's bottle	biberon [beebai**ron**]
body lotion	lozione per il corpo [lots**yo**nay pair eel **kor**po]
brush	spazzola [**spat**zola]
comb	pettine [**pet**teenay]
condom	profilattico [profee**lat**teeko]
cotton wool	ovatta [o**vat**ta]
deodorant	deodorante [dayodo**ran**tay]
detergent	detersivo [detair**see**vo]
dummy	succhietto [sook**yet**to]
elastic hairband	elastico per capelli [e**las**teeko pair ka**pel**lee]
hair gel	gel per capelli [jel pair ka**pel**lee]
hairspray	lacca per capelli [**lak**ka pair ka**pel**lee]
insect repellent	antizanzare [anteetsant**zar**ay]
nail file	limetta per le unghie [lee**met**ta pair lay **oong**yay]
nail scissors	forbici per le unghie [**for**beechee pair lay **oong**yay]
nappies	pannolini [panno**lee**nee]
perfume	profumo [pro**foo**mo]
razor-blade	lamette da barba [la**met**tay da **bar**ba]
sanitary towels	pannolini (da donna) [panno**lee**nee (da **don**na)]
saftey pin	spilla di sicurezza [**speel**la dee seekoo**ret**za]
shaving foam	schiuma da barba [**skyoo**ma da **bar**ba]
shower gel	gel per doccia [jel pair **doch**ha]
soap	sapone [sa**po**nay]
tampons	tamponi [tam**po**nee]
toilet paper	carta igienica [**kar**ta eej**yen**eeka]
tweezers	pinzetta [peent**set**ta]
toothbrush	spazzolino da denti [spatzo**lee**no da **den**tee]
toothpaste	dentifricio [dentee**free**cho]
washing-up liquid	detersivo per i piatti [detair**see**vo pair ee **pyat**tee]

When can I pick up the glasses?	Quando posso venire a prendere gli occhiali? [**kwan**do **pos**so ve**nee**ray a **pren**dairay lyee ok**kya**lee]
I'm shortsighted/ longsighted.	Io sono miope/presbite. [**ee**-o **so**no **mee**opay/**prez**beetay]
I have	**Io ho** [**ee**-o o]
lost my glasses/contact lens	perso i miei occhiali/una lente a contatto [**pair**so ee m**ya**yee ok**kya**lee/**oo**na **len**tay a kon**tat**to]
... dioptre in the right/left eye.	a destra/sinistra ... diottrie. [a **des**tra/see**nees**tra ... dee**ot**treeay]

I need	Io ho bisogno di [ee-o o beezonyo dee]
a pair of sunglasses	occhiali da sole [okkyalee da solay]
a spectacle case	un astuccio per occhiali
	[oon astoocho pair okkyalee]
a pair of binoculars	un binocolo [oon beenokolo]
cleansing solution/rinsing	una soluzione per pulire/conservare
solution	[oona solootsyonay pair pooleeray/konsairvaray]
for hard/soft contact	per lenti a contatto dure/morbide.
lenses.	[pair lentee a kontatto dooray/morbeeday]

Chemist

I'd like	Io vorrei [ee-o vorrayee]
some plasters	cerotti [chairottee]
some tissues	fazzoletti di carta [fatzolettee dee karta]
a hand/skin creme	una crema per le mani/per la pelle
	[oona krayma pair lay manee/pair la pellay]
a suntan lotion with	una crema per il sole con fattore protettivo
protection factor 6/12	sei/dodici
	[oona krayma pair eel solay kon fattoray
	protetteevo say/dodeechee]
an after sun lotion	un doposole [oon doposolay]
a shampoo	uno sciampo [oono shampo]
for normal hair	per capelli normali
	[pair kapellee normalee]
for dry hair	per capelli secchi [pair kapellee sekkee]
for greasy hair	per capelli grassi [pair kapellee grassee]
for dandruff.	contro la forfora. [kontro la forfora]

Tobacconist

... please.	..., prego [praygo]
A packet/carton of cigarettes	Un pacchetto/Una stecca di sigarette
	[oon pakketto/oona stekka dee seegarettay]
with/without filters.	con/senza filtro
	[kon/sendza feeltro]
A packet of pipe tobacco	Tabacco da pipa
	[tabakko da peepa]
A box of matches	Fiammiferi [fyammeefairee]
A lighter	Un accendino
	[oon achendeeno]

Sale e Tabacchi

The words *Sale e Tabacchi* can still sometimes be read on old-fashioned signs above tobacconists' shops. In the old days, the sale of salt was controlled by the state. Only those shops, bars and restaurants displaying the sign *Sale e* *Tabacchi* were allowed to sell salt and tobacco, both of which were highly taxed. This restriction now only applies to tobacco and stamps. Look for the sign with the large, white T on a blue background.

71

Most public phone boxes now only accept phonecards

Practical Information

Medical assistance

At the doctor's surgery

I need a doctor (urgently).

Io ho bisogno (subito) di un medico.
[ee-o o beezonyo (soobeeto) dee oon maydeeko]

Please call a doctor/an ambulance.

Prego telefoni al medico di emergenza/ad una autoambulanza. [praygo telayfonee al maydeeko dee emairjentsa/ad oona owtoamboolantsa]

Is there a ... around here?
gynaecologist
paediatrician
dentist
English-speaking

Dove trovo [dovay trovo]
un ginecologo [oon jeenaykologo]
un pediatra [oon pedyatra]
un dentista [oon denteesta]
che parla inglese?
[kay parla eenglayzay]

Can the doctor come here?

Può venire qui il medico?
[pwo veneeray kwee eel maydeeko]

When are his surgery hours?

Quando è aperto l'ambulatorio?
[kwando ay apairto lamboolatoreeo]

Can I have an appointment immediately?
When can I come?

Posso venire subito nell'ambulatorio?
[posso veneeray soobeeto nellamboolatoreeo]
Quando posso venire? [kwando posso veneeray]

* Che cosa posso fare per Lei?
[kay koza posso faray pair lay]

What can I do for you?

I feel sick (all the time).

Mi sento (continuamente) male.
[mee sento (konteenooamentay) malay]

I had a fall.

Sono caduto. [sono kadooto]

I've got	Io ho [ee-o o]
a cold	il raffreddore [eel raffred**dor**ay]
an allergy	un'allergia [oonallair**jee**a]
diarrhoea	la diarrea [la deear**ra**ya]
the flu	l'influenza [leenfloo**en**tsa]
a cough	la tosse [la **tos**say]
a headache	mal di testa [mal dee **tes**ta]
stomach-ache	mal di pancia [mal dee **pan**cha]
earache	mal di orecchi [mal dee o**rek**kee]
a sore throat	mal di gola [mal dee **go**la]
cystitis	un'infezione alla vescica [ooneenfets**yo**nay **al**la ve**shee**ka]
shooting pains in the heart	fitte al cuore [**feet**tay al **kwo**ray]
a (high) temperature.	la febbre (alta). [la **feb**bray (**al**ta)]

I have vomited. — Io ho vomitato [ee-o o vomee**ta**to]

* Quanto è alta la febbre? [**kwan**to ay **al**ta la **feb**bray] — How high is the temperature?

* Da quando ha la febbre? [da **kwan**do a la **feb**bray] — When did the fever start?

Two days ago. — Da due giorni. [da **doo**ay **jor**nee]

* Dove fa male? [**do**vay fa **ma**lay] — Where does it hurt?

* Non è niente di grave. [non ay **nyen**tay dee **gra**vay] — It's nothing serious.

Is the leg broken? — È fratturata la gamba? [ay frattoo**ra**ta la **gam**ba]

Is the arm/ the finger broken? — È fratturato il braccio/il dito? [ay frattoo**ra**to eel **bra**cho/eel **dee**to]

I've got digestion problems. — Io non digerisco il mangiare [**ee**-o non deejai**rees**ko eel man**ja**ray]

I am allergic to penicillin. — Io non sopporto la penicillina. [**ee**-o non sop**por**to la peneechee**lleena**]

I'm	Io sono [eeo sono]
pregnant/4 months pregnant	incinta/nel quarto mese di gravidanza [in**cheen**ta/nel **kwar**to **may**zay dee grave**edan**tza]
a diabetic	malato di diabete [ma**la**to dee deea**bay**tay]
chronically ill.	malato cronico *(m)*/malata cronica *(f)*. [ma**la**to **kroneeko**/ma**la**ta **kroneeka**]

Directions for use of medicine

digiuno	on an empty stomach
due/tre volte al giorno	twice/three times a day
esterno/interno	external/internal
prima/dopo i pasti	before/after food
sciogliere in acqua	dissolve in water
sciogliere in bocca	dissolve on the tongue
senza masticare	swallow whole

Could you
  prescribe this for me
  prescribe something for ...,
  please?

Mi può [mee pwo]
  prescrivere questo [pre**scree**vairai **kwes**to]
  prescrivere qualcosa contro ...?
  [pre**scree**vairay kwal**koza kon**tro]

At the dentist

I've got (terrible) toothache.

Io ho (un forte) mal di denti.
[**ee**-o o (oon **for**tay) mal dee **den**tee]

I've lost a filling.

Io ho perso una piombatura.
[**ee**-o o **pair**so **oo**na pyomba**too**ra]

Could you
  see me immediately
  give me something for the
  pain, please?

Può [pwo]
  visitarmi subito [veezee**tar**mee **soo**beeto]
  darmi un antidolorifero?
  [**dar**mee oon anteedolo**ree**fairo]

Medical assistance

aids	aids [**a**eeds]
allergy	allergia [aller**jee**a]
antibiotic	antibiotico [anteeb**yo**teeko]
appendicitis	appendicite [appendee**chee**tay]
aspirin	aspirina [aspee**ree**na]
(strong) bleeding	emorragia (forte) [emmora**jee**a (**for**tay)]
blood test	controllo del sangue [kon**trol**lo del **san**gway]
burn	bruciatura [broocha**too**ra]
certificate	certificato medico [chairteefee**ka**to **may**deeko]
circulatory problems	disturbo di circolazione [dee**stoor**bo dee cheerkolats**yo**nay]
cold	raffreddore [raffred**dor**ay]
condom	profilattico [profee**lat**teeko]
concussion	commozione cerebrale [kommots**yo**nay chairay**bra**lay]
constipation	stitichezza [steetee**kayt**za]
cough mixture	sciroppo per la tosse [shee**rop**po pair la **tos**say]
cramp	crampo [**kram**po]
eardrops	gocce per le orecchie [**go**chay pair lay o**rek**yay]
eyedrops	collirio [kol**leer**eeo]
flu	influenza [eenfloo**en**tsa]
fracture	ernia [**air**neea]
fungus (infection)	(infezione da) fungo [(eenfets**yo**nay da) **foon**go]
gastroenteritis	malattie dell'apparato digerente [malat**tee**ay dellap**pa**rato deejai**ren**tay]
HIV-positive	sieropositivo [s**yair**opoze**etee**vo]
infection	infezione [infets**yo**nay]
infectious	contagioso/-a [konta**jo**zo/-a]

Could you do a temporary repair on the tooth/the bridge/the crown.

Per favore ripari solo provvisoriamente il dente/il ponte/la corona.
[pair favoray reeparee solo proveezoreeamentay eel dentay/eel pontay/la korona]

Could you give me an/no injection, please.

Io (non) vorrei una iniezione.
[ee-o (non) vorrayee oona eenyetsyonay]

At the hospital

Where is
  the nearest hospital
  accident and emergency?

Dov'è [dovay]
  l'ospedale più vicino [l'ospedalay pyoo veecheeno]
  l'ambulanza? [lamboolantsa]

Please call
  Mr/Mrs ...
  at the ... Hotel!

Prego informi [praygo eenformee]
  il signor/la signora ... [eel seenyor/la seenyora]
  all'hotel ...! [al-otel]

inflammation	infiammazione [eenfyammatsyonay]
migraine	emicrania [emmeekranya]
ointment	unguento [oongwento]
operation	operazione [opairatsyonay]
painkiller	pillole contro il dolore [peellolay kontro eel doloray]
plaster	cerotto [chairotto]
poisoning	avvelenamento [avelaynamento]
pulled muscle	strappo muscolare [strappo mooskolaray]
pulled tendon	stiramento del tendine [steeramento del tendeenay]
pus	pus [poos]
rash	sfogo [sfogo]
seasickness	mal di mare [mal dee maray]
sleeping pills	pillole contro l'insonnia [peellolay kontro leensonya]
snakebite	morso da serpente [morso da sairpentay]
sprained	slogato/-a [slogato/-a]
sunstroke	colpo di sole [kolpo dee solay]
temperature	febbre [febbray]
tranquilizer	calmante [kalmantay]
travel sickness	malattia da viaggio [malateea da vyajjo]
vomiting	vomito [vomeeto]
vaccinate	vaccinare [vacheenaray]
vaccination	vaccinazione [vacheenatsyonay]
virus	virus [veeroos]
wound	ferita [faireeta]
x-ray	radiografia [radeeografeea]

Do you have private/two-bed rooms?

Avete camere private/camere a due letti? [avaytay kamairay preevatay/kamairay a dooay lettee]

What's the diagnosis?
Which treatment/therapy do you propose?

Qual'è la diagnosi? [kwalay la deeanyozee]
Quale terapia è necessaria? [kwalay tairapeea ay nechessareea]

How long will I have to stay?

Quanto devo rimanere? [kwanto dayvo reemanairay]

When can I get up?

(Quando) Posso alzarmi? [(kwando) posso altsarmee]

I feel (don't feel any) better.

(Non) Sto meglio. [(non) sto maylyo]

I need
a painkiller
sleeping pills.

Ho bisogno di [o beezonyo dee]
un antidolorifero [oon anteedoloreefairo]
pillole per l'insonnia. [peellolay pair leensonya]

Am I well enough to travel?

Posso viaggiare? [posso vyajjaray]

I'd like ...
to see the doctor
to be discharged
a medical report

a certificate
for my medical insurance

for my doctor.

Io vorrei [ee-o vorrayee]
parlare con il medico [parlaray kon eel maydeeko]
essere rilasciato [essairay reelashato]
un rapporto di malattia [oon rapporto dee malatteea]
un certificato [oon chairteefeekato]
per la mia cassa malattia [pair la mee-a kassa malatteea]
per il mio medico di fiducia. [pair eel mee-o maydeeko dee feedoocha]

At the pharmacy

I'm looking for a pharmacy.

Io cerco una farmacia [ee-o chairko oona farmacheea]

I have (I don't have) a prescription.

Io (non) ho una ricetta. [ee-o (non) o oona reechetta]

I need
some plasters
an insect repellent

something for a cough/
for a (head) ache
for me
for adults/for children.

Io ho bisogno di [ee-o o beezonyo dee]
cerotti [chairottee]
qualcosa contro le zanzare [kwalkoza kontro lay tzantzaray]
qualcosa contro la tosse/il dolore (di testa) [kwalkoza kontro la tossay/eel doloray (dee testa)]
per me [pair may]
per adulti/bambini. [pair adooltee/bambeenee]

Is the medicine strong/weak?

Questa medicina è forte/leggero? [kwesto medeecheena ay fortay/lejairo]

How many tablets/drops do I have to take?

Quante pastiglie/gocce devo prendere? [kwantay pasteelyay/gochay dayvo prendairay]

Could you give me a receipt/a copy of the prescription, please!

Prego mi dia una ricevuta/una copia della ricetta. [praygo mee deea oona reechayvoota/oona kopya della reechetta]

Holidays and festivals

Is there a (national) holiday today?
Oggi è festa (nazionale)?
[ojjee ay festa (natsyonalay)]

What's being celebrated today?
Quale festa si festeggia oggi?
[kwalay festa see festejja ojjee]

When does the festival start?
Quando comincia il programma festivo?
[kwando komeencha eel programma festeevo]

How long does it last?
Quanto dura? [kwanto doora]

Where does the festival take place?
Dove si fa la manifestazione?
[dovay see fa la maneefestatsyonay]

Money matters

Can I pay with ... here?
Posso pagare con
[posso pagaray kon]

cheques
assegno [assenyo]

traveller's cheques
traveller's cheques [travellers sheks]

my cheque card
carta assegni [karta assenyee]

credit card
carta di credito? [karta dee kraydeeto]

Where's the nearest
Dov'è/C'è [dovay/chay]

bank
una banca [oona banka]

bureau de change
un ufficio di cambio
[oon oofeecho dee kambyo]

cash dispenser?
un bancomat? [oon bankomat]

What time does the bank close?
Quando/Fino a quando è aperta la banca?
[kwando/feeno a kwando ay apairta la banka]

* Quanto desidera?
[kwanto deseedaira]
How much do you want?

300 000 lire.
Trecentomila lire. [traychentomeela leeray]

What's the current exchange rate?
Quanto è il cambio attuale? [kwanto ay eel kambyo attwalay]

What's the maximum amount per cheque?
Quanto è la somma massima per assegno?
[kwanto ay la somma masseema pair assenyo]

I'd like to change 100 pounds sterling/dollars into lire, please.
Io vorrei cambiare cento sterline/dollari in Lire.
[ee-o vorrayee kambyaray chento stairleenay/dollaree een leeray]

Please give me small notes/some coins as well!
Mi dia per favore biglietti di piccolo taglio/anche moneta! [mee deea pair favoray beelyettee dee peekolo talyo/ankay monayta]

Can I use my credit card to get cash?
Posso avere soldi con la mia carta di credito?
[posso avairay soldee kon la mee-a karta dee kraydeeto]

* Il Suo assegno prego.
[eel soo-o assenyo praygo]
Can I see your cheque card, please?

* Prego firmi qui
[praygo feermee kwee]
Sign here, please.

* Prego dia il Suo numero di codice! [**pray**go **dee**a eel **soo**-o **noo**mairo dee **ko**deechay]

Enter your pin number, please!

Has my bank transfer/money order arrived yet?

È arrivato il vaglia bancario dalla mia banca/ il vaglia postale dal mio ufficio postale? [ay arree**va**to eel **val**ya ban**kar**yo **dal**la **mee**-a **ban**ka/ eel **val**ya postalay dal **mee**-o oo**fee**echo postalay]

Crime and police

Where's the nearest police station?

Dov'è la prossima stazione di polizia? [do**vay** la **pros**seema stats**yo**ne dee poleet**see**a]

Please call the police!

Prego telefoni alla polizia! [**pray**go te**lay**fone **al**la poleet**see**a]

I've been
  robbed
  mugged on the road/
  at the beach.

Sono stato/stata [sono stato/stata]
  derubato/derubata [dairoo**ba**to/dairoo**ba**ta]
  aggredito/aggredita sulla strada/
  sulla spiaggia. [agray**dee**to/agray**dee**ta **sool**la **stra**da/**sool**la spy**aj**ja]

This man is bothering/following me.

Questo uomo mi dà fastidio/mi segue. [**kwes**to **wo**mo mee da fas**teed**yo/mee **say**gway]

My car has been broken into.

La mia macchina è stata scassinata. [la **mee**-a **mak**keena ay **sta**ta skasseenata]

... has been stolen!

È stato rubato/stata rubata [ay **sta**to roo**ba**to/**sta**ta roo**ba**ta]

  My passport

la mia carta di identità [la **mee**-a **kar**ta dee eedenteeta]

  My car/bicycle

la mia macchina/bicicletta [la **mee**-a **mak**keena/beecheekletta]

  My wallet

il mio portafoglio [eel **mee**-o porta**fol**yo]

  My camera

la mia macchina fotografica [la **mee**-a **mak**keena fotografeeka]

  My handbag

la mia borsa [la **mee**-a **bor**sa]

  My cheques/
  My cheque card

i miei assegni/la mia carta assegni [ee **my**ayee assen**yee**/la **mee**-a **kar**ta assen**yee**]

  My watch

il mio orologio. [eel **mee**-o oro**lo**jo]

I'd like to report
  a theft
  a fraud
  a robbery
  a rape

Io vorrei denunciare [**ee**o vor**ray**ee denoon**char**ay]
  un furto [oon **foor**to]
  un imbroglio [oon eem**brol**yo]
  un'aggressione [oonagress**yo**nay]
  uno stupro [**oo**no **stoo**pro]

I'd like to
  report an accident

  speak to a lawyer/
  call my embassy

Io vorrei [**ee**-o vor**ray**ee]
  riferire un incidente [reefairee**ray** dee oon eencheedentay]
  parlare con un avvocato/con la mia ambasciata [parla**ray** kon oon avo**ka**to/ kon la **mee**-a amba**sha**ta]

Opening times

Shops are open Monday to Saturday from 9am to 1pm and from 4pm to 7pm. Many boutiques close on Monday morning. Banks open Monday to Friday from 8.30am to 1pm and again from 2.45pm to 3.45pm.

The *siesta* break from 1pm to 4pm is a long-established nationwide tradition.

During these hours, most things come to a standstill (except for in the big towns and cities where the siesta is slowly becoming a thing of the past).

When planning your trip to Italy, it's worth remembering that the whole country takes its summer holiday in August and many public services close.

Does anyone here speak English?
C'è qualcuno che parla inglese?
[chay kwal**koo**no kay **par**la eenglayzay]

I need
an interpreter
a written document for insurance purposes.
Io ho bisogno di [ee-o o bee**zon**yo dee]
un interprete [oon een**tair**pretay]
un certificato per la mia assicurazione. [oon chairteefee**ka**to pair la **mee**-a asseekoorats**yo**nay]

It wasn't my fault
Io non ho colpa. [ee-o non o **kol**pa]

I've got nothing to do with it
Io non ho niente a che vedere.
[ee-o non o n**yen**tay a kay ve**dair**ay]

* Quando/Dove è successo?
[**kwan**do/**do**vay ay soo**chess**o]
When/Where did it happen?

Emergencies

▶ (See also breakdown, accident, page 25, and at the hospital, page 75)

* Attenzione! [attents**yo**nay]
* Pericolo (di morte)!
[pai**ree**kolo dee (**mor**tay)]
* Uscita di emergenza
[u**shee**ta dee emair**jayn**tsa]
Caution!
Danger (of death)!

Emergency exit

Help!
Aiuto! [a**yoo**to]/Soccorso! [sok**kor**so]

Opening times

When does ... open/close?
the supermarket
the shop
the bank
the post office
the museum?
Quando apre/chiude [**kwan**do apray/**kyoo**day]
il supermercato [eel soopairmair**ka**to]
il negozio [eel ne**gots**yo]
la banca [la **ban**ka]
l'ufficio postale [loo**fee**cho posta**lay**]
il museo? [eel moo**zay**o]

Are you closed at lunch time?
Ha aperto a mezzogiorno?
[a a**pair**to a metzo**jor**no]

Is there a day you are closed?
Ha un giorno di riposo?
[a oon **jor**no dee ree**po**zo]

Post office

Where can I find
a post office
a post-box?

Per favore dov'è [pair favoray dovay]
l'ufficio postale [loofeecho postalay]
una cassetta postale? [oona kassetta postalay]

I'd like
some/10 stamps/
special issue stamps
for postcards/letters
to England/the United
States
a phonecard.

Io vorrei [ee-o vorrayee]
di francobolli/una serie speciale
[dee frankobollee/oona sairyay spechalay]
per cartoline/lettere [pair kartoleenay/lettairay]
per l'Inghilterra/per gli Stati Uniti [pair
leengeeltairra/pair lyee statee ooneetee)]
una carta telefonica. [oona karta telayfoneeka]

By airmail.
Express, please.

Per via aerea, prego. [pair veea a-airea praygo]
Per espresso, prego. [pair espresso praygo]

* Fermo posta. [**fairmo posta**]

Poste restante.

Do you have any mail for me?
My name is ...

C'è posta per me? [chay posta pair may]
Il mio nome è ... [eel mee-o nomay ay]

I would like to send a packet/
a telegram.

Io vorrei mandare un pacchetto/un telegramma.
[ee-o vorrayee mandaray oon paketto/oon
telegramma]

How much do you charge for
ten words?

Quanto costano dieci parole?
[kwanto kostano dyaychee parolay]

I'd like to make a phone call
to England.
Can I call direct?

Vorrei telefonare in Inghilterra/negli Stati Uniti.
[vorrayee telefonaray een eengeeltairra]
Posso telefonare direttamente?
[posso telefonaray deerettamentay]

▶ (See also telecommunications, page 82)

Can I send a fax to ... from
here?

Si può mandare da qui un telefax a ...?
[see pwo mandaray da kwee oon telefax a]

How much is it?

Quanto costa? [kwanto kosta]

*Vatican City
postboxes are blue
instead of the
usual red seen in
the rest of Italy*

Radio and television

On which wavelength can I pick up
the traffic report

English radio programmes?

Da quale frequenza si può ricevere
[da **kwa**lay fre**kwen**tsa see pwo ree**chay**vairay]
il programma sul traffico
[eel pro**gram**ma sool **traf**feeko]
i programmi in inglese?
[ee pro**gram**mee een een**glay**zay]

What time is the news?

A che ora ci sono le notizie?
[a kay **o**ra chee **so**no lay no**teets**yay]

Do you have a TV guide?

Ha un giornale con i programmi televisivi?
[a oon jor**na**lay kon ee pro**gram**mee telayvee**zee**vee]

What channels do you get?

Quali canali ricevono?
[**kwa**lee ka**na**lee see ree**chay**vono]

Telecommunications

(Where) can I
make a phone call
buy a phonecard?

(Dove) Posso [(**do**vay) **pos**so]
telefonare [telayfo**na**ray]
comprare una carta telefonica?
[kom**pra**ray **oo**na **kar**ta telay**fon**eeka]

Can I send an e-mail (from here)?

Posso mandare un e-mail da qui? [**pos**so man**da**ray oon e-mail (da kwee)]

Is there ... near here?
a phone box
a public phone
a payphone/cardphone

a cyber café

C'è ... da queste parti [chay da **kwes**tay **par**tee]
una cabina telefonica [**oo**na ka**bee**na telay**fon**eeka]
un telefono pubblico [oon te**lay**fono **poo**bleeko]
un telefono a gettoni/con tessera
[oon te**lay**fono a jet**to**nee/kon **tes**saira]
un cyber café [oon **sy**ber kaf**fay**]

Can you change this?

Per favore può cambiare?
[pair fa**vo**ray pwo kamb**ya**ray]

I need coins for the telephone.

Ho bisogno di moneta per telefonare.
[o bee**zon**yo dee mo**nay**ta pair telefo**na**ray]

Do you have a phonebook for ...?
Can I dial direct to ...?

Posso avere un elenco telefonico di ... ?
[**pos**so a**vai**ray oon e**len**ko telay**fon**eeko dee]
Posso telefonare direttamente a ...?
[**pos**so telayfo**na**ray deeretta**men**tay a]

A long-distance call to ..., please!
How long do I have to wait?
What's the charge per minute to ...?
Is there a cheap rate at night time?
I'd like to make a reversed charge call.

Prego una telefonata interurbana a ...!
[**pray**go **oo**na telayfo**na**ta eentairoor**ba**na a]
Quanto devo aspettare? [**kwan**to **day**vo aspet**ta**ray]
Quanto costa un minuto per ...?
[**kwan**to **kos**ta oon mee**noo**to pair]
C'è una tariffa economica notturna?
[chay **oo**na ta**reef**fa ekono**mee**ka not**toor**na]
Io vorrei annunciare una telefonata a carico del ricevente [**ee**-o vor**ray**ee anoon**char**ay **oo**na telefo**na**ta a ka**ree**ko del reechev**en**tay]

* Occupato. [okkoo**pa**to]
* Non risponde nessuno.
[non rees**pon**day nes**soo**no]

Engaged.
There's no reply.

Making phone calls

In addition to the telephone offices run by the national telephone company, Telecom, there are phone boxes everywhere. Most of these now only accept phonecards (scheda/carta telefonica), but some still take gettoni (tokens) and coins (100, 200 or 500 lira).

Phonecards to the value of 5,000 or 10,000 lira and gettoni (200 lira) can be bought from tobacconists and Telecom offices.

The international dialling code for the United Kingdom is 00 44, the Republic of Ireland 00 353 and the United States 00 1.

The following numbers are free of charge: police: 113; fire brigade: 112; information: 110.

Hello!	Pronto! [**pron**to]
Who's calling?	Chi parla? [kee **par**la]
This is ...	Qui parla ... [kwee **par**la]
Can I speak to Mr/Mrs ... ?	Posso parlare con il signor/la signora ...? [**pos**so parla**ray** kon eel seen**yor**/la seen**yor**a]
* Sono io. [**so**no ee-o]	Speaking.
* Lui/Lei purtroppo non è qui. [**loo**-ee/lay poor**trop**po non ay kwee]	Sorry, he/she is not here at the moment.
Do you speak English?	Lei parla inglese? [lay **par**la een**glay**zay]
When can I speak to him/her?	Quando si può parlare con lui/lei? [**kwan**do see pwo par**lar**ay kon **loo**-ee/lay]
Please tell him/her that I called.	Gli/le Dica per favore che io ho telefonato. [lyee/lay **dee**ka pair fa**vor**ay kay ee-o o telefo**na**to]
My number is ...	Il mio numero è ... [eel **mee**-o **noo**mairo ay]
Thanks, good-bye.	Grazie, a risentirci! [**grats**yay a reesen**teer**chee]

Toilets

Where are the toilets please?	Dove sono i gabinetti per favore? [**do**vay **so**no ee gabee**net**tee pair fa**vor**ay]
Is there a public toilet around here?	Ci sono gabinetti pubblici qui vicino? [chee **so**no gabee**net**tee **poo**bleechee kwee vee**chee**no]
* Donne/Uomini [**don**nay/**wom**meenee]	Ladies/Gentlemen

Tipping

Is service included?	Il servizio è compreso nel prezzo? [eel sair**veets**yo ay kom**pray**zo nel **pret**zo]
How much does one tip?	Quant'è la mancia di solito? [kwan**tay** la **man**cha dee so**lee**to]
That's for you!	Questo è per Lei! [**kwes**to ay pair lay]
Keep the change!	Tenga pure il resto! [**ten**ga **poor**ay eel **res**to]
That's fine!	Va bene così! [va **bay**nay ko**zee**]

English–Italian A–Z

A

accident incidente [eencheedentay] 25, 79, 80

accommodation alloggio [allojo] 32

address indirizzo [eendeereetzo] 15, 27

admission ticket biglietto di entrata [beelyetto dee entrata] 49, 57

adult adulto [adoolto] 29, 77

age età [eta] 14

agreed d'accordo [dakkordo]

air conditioning aria condizionata [aarya kondeetsyonata] 26, 38

air mattress materasso pneumatico [matairasso pnayoomateeko] 53

air aria [aarya]

aircraft aereo [a-airayo] 30

airport aeroporto [a-airoporto] 30

alarm clock sveglia [svelya] 66

alcohol level (parts per thousand) quantità pair mille [kwanteeta pair meellay]

all tutti [toottee]

alone solo/-a [solo/-a]

ambulance ambulanza [amboolantsa] 25, 75, 80

America l'America [amaireeka] 13

American americano [amereekano] 13

angry furioso/-a [fooreeozo/-a]

animal animale [aneemalay] 35

anorak anorak [anorak] 67

answering machine segreteria telefonica [segretairee-a telayfoneeka] 82

antiques antichità [anteekeeta] 69

apology scusa [skooza] 13

appointment appuntamento [appoontamento] 14

arena arena [arayna] 50

arm braccio [bracho] 73

art gallery galleria d'arte [gallaireea dartay] 50

aunt zia [tseea] 13

Australia l'Australia [owstralya] 13

Australian australiano [owstralyano] 13

autumn autunno [owtoonno] 17

avenue viale [vee-alay]

B

baby food alimenti per neonati [aleementee pair nayonatee] 62

baby neonato [nayonato]

baby's bottle biberon [beebairon] 71

bachelor scapolo [skappolo] 14, 15

back indietro [eendyaytro]

bad cattivo/-a [katteevo/-a]

bakery panetteria [panettaireea] 61

ball palla [palla] 55

bank holiday giorno di festa [jorno dee festa] 78

bank banca [banka] 78

bar cantina [kanteena] 58

bath bagno [banyo] 33, 53

battery batteria [battaireea] 26, 66, 67

bay baia [baya] 53

beach spiaggia [spyajja] 33, 53

beautiful bello/-a [bello/-a]

beauty (salon) (salone di) cosmetica [(salonay dee) kozmeteeka] 71

bed letto [letto] 32, 38

bedcover coperta [kopairta] 38

beer birra [beerra] 48

beginning inizio [eeneetsyo]

behind indietro [eendyaytro]

belt cintura [cheentoora] 67

bicycle bicicletta [beecheekletta] 22

bikini bikini [beekeenee] 67

bill conto [konto]

birthday compleanno [komplayanno] 14

black nero/-a [nairo/-a] 20

blame colpa [kolpa]

blood sangue [sangway] 72

blouse camicetta [kameechetta] 65

boat barca [barka] 53, nave [navay] 31

body (lotion) (lozione per il) corpo [(lotsyonay pair eel) korpo] 71

book libro [leebro] 65

bookshop libreria [leebraireea] 65

boots stivali [steevalee] 67

border confini [konfeenee] 21

boring noioso [noyozo]

born nato/-a [nato/-a]

bottle opener apribottiglia [apreebotteelya] 61

bottle bottiglia [bot**teel**ya] 43, 64
bowl terrina [tair**reena**]
boy ragazzo [ra**gatzo**]
boy-friend amico [a**meeko**] 13, 14
bra reggiseno [rejee**sayno**] 67
breakdown panne [**pannay**] 25, 79, 80
breakfast colazione [kolatsy**onay**] 33, 41, 44
bridge ponte [**pontay**] 50, 75
briefcase portafoglio [porta**folyo**] 79
broken rotto/-a [**rotto/-a**]
brooch spilla [**speella**] 66
brother fratello [fra**tello**] 13
brother-in-law cognato [kon**yato**] 13
bureau de change cambio [**kambyo**] 78
bus autobus [**owtoboos**] 28, 29
bus station stazione dei pullman [stats**yonay dayee poolman**] 28, 29
bus-stop fermata [fair**mata**] 28, 29
butcher macelleria [machellai**reea**] 61
button bottone [bot**tonay**]
buy [vb] comprare [kom**praray**] 61

C

cabin (boat) cabina [ka**beena**] 31
cabin (on a camp-site) capanna [ka**panna**] 37
café caffè [ka**ffay**] 40
cake-shop pasticceria [pastee**chaireea**] 61
camera macchina fotografica [**makkeena** fotogra**feeka**] 67, 69
camper van camper [**kampair**] 22, 37
camp-site campeggio [kam**payjo**] 37
cap berretto [bai**retto**] 67
car auto [**owto**]; macchina [**makkeena**] 22, 24
caravan roulotte [roo**lott**] 37
car-park parcheggio [par**kayjo**] 23, 33
cash contanti [kon**tantee**] 78
cash-desk cassa [**kassa**] 57, 61
castle castello [kas**tello**] 50,51
cat gatto [**gatto**] 35
cathedral cattedrale [kattay**dralay**] 50
cause causa [**kausa**]; motivo [mo**teevo**]
centimetre centimetro [chen**teemetro**] 19
centre centro [**chentro**] 22
certificate certificato [chairteefee**kato**] 77, 79
chain catena [ka**tayna**] 26
chair sedia [**saydya**]

charges spese [**spay**zay]
charter flight volo charter [**volo charter**] 30
cheap economico [eko**nomeeko**]
cheeky impertinente [eempairtee**nayntay**]
chemist farmacia [farma**cheea**] 77
cheque assegno [as**senyo**] 33, 78
child bambino [bam**beeno**] 29, 42, 77
church chiesa [**kyayza**] 50
cigarette sigarette [seega**rettay**] 71
cinema cinema [**cheenayma**] 57
circular tour giro turistico [**jeero** too**reesteeko**] 49, 52
city centre centro [**chentro**] 22
clean pulito/-a [poo**leeto/-a**]
cleaning pulizia [pooleet**seea**] 66
clear chiaro/-a [**kyaro/-a**]
clock orologio [oro**lojo**] 66, 79
closed chiuso/-a [**kyoozo/-a**] 80
clothing abbigliamento [abbeelya**mento**] 65
coast costa [**kosta**] 53
coat cappotto [kap**potto**] 67
coins monete [mo**naytay**] 39, 78, 82
cold freddo/-a [**freddo/-a**]
collar colletto [kol**letto**] 65
colour colore [ko**loray**] 20
comb pettine [**petteenay**] 71
compartment scompartimento [skompartee**mento**] 29
compensation risarcimento danni [reesarchee**mento dannee**]
complaint lagnanza [lan**yantsa**] 34, 42
concert concerto [kon**chairto**] 57
condom profilattico [profee**latteeko**] 71
connecting (flight/train) coincidenza (per l'aereo/treno) [koeenchee**dentsa** (pair la-**ayrayo/trayno**)] 29, 30
connection collegamento [kollega**mento**] 28, 30
consulate consolato [kon**solato**] 79
contraceptive anticoncezionali [anteekonchetsy**onalee**] 72, 77
contract contratto [kon**tratto**]
cook [f] cuoca [**kwokka**] 40
cook [m] cuoco [**kwokko**] 40
cooked cucinato/-a [koochee**nato/-a**]
corkscrew cavatappi [kava**tappee**] 61
corner angolo [**angolo**]
cost [vb] assaggiare [assa**jaray**]
cotton buds bastoncini di ovatta [baston**cheenee dee ovatta**] 71

cotton wool ovatta [ovatta] 71
cotton cotone [kotonay] 66
counter sportello [sportello] 29, 57
country house tenuta [tenoota];
  possedimento rurale
  [possedeemento ruralay] 32
country road strada provinciale
  [strada proveenchalay] 22
country paese [pa-ayzay]
court tribunale [treeboonalay]
cousin *[f]* cugina [koojeena] 13
cousin *[m]* cugino [koojeeno] 13
credit card carta di credito
  [karta dee kraydeeto] 33, 78
cruise crociera [krochaira] 31
culture cultura [kooltoora] 57
cup tazza [tatza] 43
currency valuta [valoota] 78
customs dogana [dogana] 21
cutlery posate [pozatay] 38, 43

D

dance *[vb]* ballare [ballaray] 59
dangerous pericolo
  [paireekolo] 23, 54, 80
dark scuro/-a [skooro/-a] 20
date data [data] 17
daughter figlia [feelya] 13
day giorno [jorno] 12, 15, 19
day-ticket carta del giorno
  [karta del jorno] 28
dear caro/-a [karo/-a]
debt debito [daybeeto]
deep profondo/-a [profondo/-a]
degree grado [grado] 20, 73
delicatessen delicatezza
  [deleekatetza] 40
dentist dentista [denteesta] 72, 74
deodorant deodorante
  [dayodorantay] 71
departure partenza [partentsa] 28, 31
deposit cauzione [kowtsyonay] 23
dessert dessert [dessair] 47
destination meta [mayta] 54
dialling code prefisso [prefeesso] 82
die morire [moreeray]
diesel diesel [deezel] 24
difference differenza [deeffairentsa]
different diverso/-a [deevairso/-a]
difficult difficile [deeffeecheelay]
direct flight volo diretto
  [volo deeretto] 30
direction direzione [deeretsyonay] 22

directly diretto [deeretto]
director direttore [deerettoray] 32, 57
dirty sporco/-a [sporko/-a]
discotheque discoteca [deeskotayka] 58
discount sconto [skonto] 61
dismissal congedo [konjaydo] 12
display window vetrina
  [vetreena] 61
diversion deviazione
  [deveeatsyonay] 23
dizzy (to feel) avere le vertigini
  [avairay lay vairteejeenee] 72
doctor medico [maydeeko] 72
dog cane [kanay] 35
donkey asino [azeeno]
door porta [porta]
double doppio [doppyo]
doubt dubbio [doobbyo]
drink *(noun)* bevanda [bevanda] 48
drinking water acqua potabile
  [akwa potabeelay] 29, 39, 48
driver autista [owteesta]; conducente
  [kondoochentay] 28, 29
driving licence patente di guida
  [patentay dee gweeda] 21, 79
drunk ubriaco/-a [oobreeako/-a]
dummy succhiotto [sookkyotto] 71

E

earrings orecchini [orekkeenee] 66
earth terra [tairra]
east est [est]; oriente [oreeayntay] 22
easy leggero/-a [lejairo/-a]
eat mangiare [manjaray] 40, 43
edible mangiabile [manjabeelay]
education educazione [edookatsyonay]
electrical store negozio di
  elettrodomestici [negotsyo dee
  elettrodomaysteechee] 67
embassy ambasciata [ambashata] 79
emergency brake freno di emergenza
  [frayno dee emairjayntsa] 29
emergency exit uscita di emergenza
  [usheeta dee emairjayntsa] 58
emergency phone colonna per
  chiamata di soccorso [kolonna pair
  kyamata di sokkorso]
empty vuoto/-a [vwoto/-a]
engaged occupato/-a [okkoopato/-a]
engine motore [motoray] 26, 27
England Inghilterra [eengeeltairra] 13
English inglese [eenglayzay] 13
enter avanti [avantee]

entertainment trattenimento
  [tratteneemento] 57
entrance entrata [entrata] 49, 57
environment ambiente [ambyentay] 54
environmental protection protezione
  ecologica [protetsyonay ekolojeeka] 54
estate agent (mediatore di) immobili
  [(medyatoray dee) eemmobeelee]
evening sera [saira] 12, 19
events (calender of) (calendario delle)
  manifestazioni [(kalendaree-o dellay)
  maneefestatsyonee] 49
everything tutto [tootto]
excursion escursione [eskoorsyonay] 52
exhausted esaurito/-a [esowreeto/-a]
exit uscita [usheeta] 23, 29
expensive caro/-a [karo/-a]

F

factory fabbrica [fabbreeka]
faithful fedele [fedaylay]
family famiglia [fameelya] 13
fan belt cinghia [cheengya] 26, 67
far lontano/-a [lontano/-a]
fashion moda [moda] 65
fast veloce [velochay]
father padre [padray] 13
faulty difetto/-a [deefetto/-a]
fax telefax [telayfax] 35, 82
fear paura [powra] 72, 79
fee tariffa [tareeffa] 78
ferry traghetto [tragetto] 31
festival festa [faysta] 78
few poco [poko]
field campo [kampo] 54
finger dito [deeto] 73
fire brigade pompiere [pompyairay] 80
fire extinguisher estintore
  [esteentoray] 80
fire fuoco [fwokko]; incendio
  [eenchendyo] 80
firm fermo/-a [fairmo/-a]
firm (company) ditta [deetta]
fishmonger pescheria [peskaireea] 64
flat appartamento [appartamento] 35
flea market mercatino delle pulci
  [mairkateeno dellay poolchee] 61
flight volo [volo] 30
flirt [vb] flirtare [fleertaray]]
floor pavimento [paveemento]
flower fiore [fyoray] 61
fly mosche [moskay]
food viveri [veevairee] 62, 64

foot piede [pyayday] 73
football calcio [kalcho] 54, 56
foreigner straniero [stranyairo] 14, 21
forest foresta [forresta] 54
fork forchetta [forketta] 43
form modulo [modoolo] 21, 79
fragile fragile [frajeelay]
free of charge gratuitamente
  [gratooeetamentay]
free libero/-a [leebairo/-a]
French francese [franchayzay] 13
fresh fresco/-a [fresko/-a]
Friday venerdì [venairdee] 17
fruit frutta [frootta] 62
full board pensione completa
  [pensyonay kompletta] 33
full up sazio/-a [satsyo/-a]
full pieno/-a [pyayno/-a]
fun divertimento [deevairteemento] 57
furniture shop mobilificio
  [mobeeleefeecho] 61
furniture mobili [mobeelee] 61
fuse valvola di sicurezza
  [valvola dee seekooretza] 26

G

garage garage [garajay] 23, 33, 38
garden giardino [jardeeno] 50
garment vestito [vesteeto] 65
gentlemen signori [seenyoree]
gents' toilet uomini [womeenee] 83
genuine vero [vairo];
  genuino [jenooeeno]
girl ragazza [ragatza]
girl-friend amica [ameeka] 13, 14
gladly volentieri [volentyairee]
glass vetro [vetro]; (tumbler) bicchiere
  [beekkyairay] 43, 50
glasses occhiali [okkyalee] 69
glove guanti [gwantee] 67
good bene [baynay]
government governo [govairno]
gram grammo [grammo] 19, 64
grandchild nipote [neepotay] 13
grandfather nonno [nonno] 13
grandmother nonna [nonna] 13
grass erba [airba]
greengrocer's fruttivendolo
  [frootteevendolo] 61
grocer's drogheria
  [drogaireea] 70
ground-floor piano terra
  [pyano tairra] 32

H

group gruppo [**groo**po]
guarantee garanzia [garant**see**a] 22, 61
guard controllore
[kontrol**lo**ray] 28, 29
guesthouse pensione
[pens**yo**nay] 32, 39
guide guida [**gwee**da] 49, 52

H

hair capelli [ka**pel**lee]
hair-brush spazzola per capelli
[**spa**tzola pair ka**pel**lee] 71
hairdresser parrucchiere
[parrook**kyai**ray]
hairspray lacca per capelli
[**la**kka pair ka**pel**lee] 71
half mezzo [**me**tzo]
hand-bag borsetta [bor**set**ta] 69, 79
handicrafts artigianato artistico
[arteeja**na**to ar**tees**teeko] 69
hand-luggage bagaglio a mano
[ba**gal**yo a **ma**no] 30
hand-towel fazzoletto
[fatzo**let**to] 38
happy felice [fe**lee**chay]
hard duro/-a [**doo**ro/-a]
hat cappello [ka**pel**lo] 67
head testa [**tes**ta] 73
healthy sano/-a [**sa**no/-a]
heating riscaldamento
[reeskalda**men**to] 38
heavy pesante [pe**zan**tay]
Help! Soccorso! [sok**kor**so] 25, 80
Help! Aiuto! [ay**oo**to] 79, 80
high alto/-a [**al**to/-a]
hobby hobby [**ob**bee]
holiday villa casa per le vacanze
[**ka**za pair lay va**kan**tsay] 35
holiday vacanze [va**kan**tsay]
home domicilio [domee**chee**lyo] 13
homeland patria [**pa**treea] 13
home-made fatto in casa
[**fat**to een **ka**za]
hope [*vb*] sperare [spai**ra**ray]
hospital ospedale [ospe**da**lay] 74
hot caldo/-a [**kal**do/-a]
hotel room camera [**ka**maira] 32
hotel hotel [o**tel**] 32
hour ora [**o**ra] 19
house casa [**ka**za] 35
household goods articoli da casa
[ar**tee**kolee da **ka**za] 61
hovercraft hovercraft [hover**craft**] 31

humid umido/-a [**oo**meedo/-a]
hunger fame [**fa**may] 40
husband marito [ma**ree**to] 13
hydrofoil aliscafo [alee**ska**fo] 31

I

identity card carta d'identità
[**kar**ta deeden**tee**ta] 21, 79
ill malato/-a [**ma**lato/-a]
important importante [impor**tan**tay]
impossible impossibile
[imposse**bee**lay]
inclusive incluso [een**kloo**zo]
information informazione
[eenformats**yo**nay] 29, 49
inhabitant abitante [abee**tan**tay]
injured ferito/-a [fai**ree**to/-a] 25, 72
innocent innocente [eenno**chen**tay]
insurance assicurazione
[asseekoorats**yo**nay] 22
intelligent intelligente [eentellee**jen**tay]
interesting interessante
[eentaires**san**tay] 52
invalid non valido/-a
[non va**lee**do/-a]
investigation esame [e**za**may] 72, 79
invoice conto [**kon**to] 39, 43
Ireland l'Irlanda [eer**lan**da]
Irish irlandese [eerlan**day**zay]
island isola [**ee**zola] 50

J

jacket giacca [**jak**ka] 65, 67
jellyfish medusa [me**doo**za] 53, 72
jeweller gioielliere [joyell**yai**ray] 66
jewellery gioielli [jo**yel**lee] 66, 69
job professione [professi**yo**nay] 14
journey viaggio [**vyaj**jo]
jumper pullover [**pool**lover] 65
junk shop rigattiere
[reegatt**yai**ray] 61, 69
justice giudizio [joo**deet**syo]

K

key chiave [**kya**vay] 39
kilo chilo [**kee**lo] 19, 64
kilometre chilometro
[**kee**lometro] 19, 23
kiosk chiosco [**kyos**ko] 61
kiss bacio [**ba**cho]
knife coltello [kol**tel**lo] 43
knitwear maglieria
[malyai**ree**a] 67

L

ladies' toilet donne [donnay] 71, 83
lady signora [seenyora]
landing sbarco [sbarko]; atterraggio
  [attairrajjo] 30
landlord oste [ostay] 40
landscape panorama [panorama] 51
language lingua [leengwa] 13
large grande [granday]
laundry lavanderia [lavandaireea] 66
lazy pigro/-a [peegro/-a]
leather goods articoli di pelle
  [arteekolee dee pellay] 69
leather pelle [pellay] 66
left luggage office deposito bagagli
  [depozeeto bagalyee]
left sinistra [seeneestra]
leg gamba [gamba] 73
length lunghezza [loongetza] 19
letter lettera [lettaira] 65, 81
letter-box cassetta per lettera
  [kassetta pair lettaira] 81
lifebelt salvagente
  [salvajentay] 31, 53
lifeboat battello di salvataggio
  [battello dee salvatajjo] 31, 53
life-jacket giubbotto di salvataggio
  [joobbotto dee salvatajjo] 31, 55
lift ascensore [ashensoray] 38
light luce [loochay] 34, 39
lightning fulmine [foolmeenay] 20, 69
linen lino [leeno] 66
lip-stick rossetto [rossetto] 71
litre litro [leetro] 19, 64
little (a) (un) poco [(oon) poko]
live [vb] vivere [veevairay]
locker cassetta di sicurezza
  [kassetta dee seekooretza] 29
long lungo [loongo]
lorry camion [kamyon] 23
lost property office ufficio degli
  oggetti smarriti [ooffeecho delyee
  ojettee zmarreetee] 79
lounger sedia a sdraio
  [sedya a zdrayo] 53
love [vb] amare [amaray]
low basso/-a [basso/-a]
luggage bagaglio [bagalyo] 29, 32, 38
lunch pranzo [prandzo] 34, 40

M

magazine rivista [reeveesta] 65
make-up trucco [trooko] 71

man uomo [womo] 13
many molto [molto]
map carta geografica
  [karta jeografeeka] 49
market hall mercato coperto
  [mairkato kopairto] 61
market mercato [mairkato] 51, 61, 64
marriage matrimonio [matreemonyo]
married couple coppia sposata
  [koppya spozata] 13
married sposato/-a [spozato/-a] 14, 15
mass (church) messa [messa]
matches fiammiferi [fyammeefairee] 71
material stoffa [stoffa] 66
meal pasto [pasto] 40
medication medicina
  [medeecheena] 73
memory ricordo [reekordo]
menu menù [menoo] 44
metre metro [metro] 19
midday mezzogiorno
  [metzojorno] 17, 19
minute minuto [meenooto] 19
misfortune disgrazia
  [deesgratsya] 25, 80
miss signorina [seenyoreena] 12
mistake (by) per sbaglio [pair zbalyo]
mistake errore [airroray] 25, 79
misunderstanding equivoco
  [ekweevoko]
modern moderno/-a [modairno/-a]
moment momento [momento] 14
monastery convento [konvento] 51
Monday lunedì [loonaydee] 17
money soldi [soldee] 78
month mese [mayzay] 17
morning (in the) il mattino
  [eel matteeno] 12, 15
morning mattina [matteena] 19
mosquito net mo rete per le mosche
  [rettay pair lay moskay]
mosquito repellent rimedio
  antizanzare [reemedyo
  anteetzantzaray] 71, 77
mosquito zanzara [tzantzara]
mother madre [madray] 13
motor-cycle moto [moto] 22
mountain montagna
  [montanya] 50
Mr signore [seenyoray] 12
much molto [molto]
museum museo [moozayo] 51
music musica [moozeeka] 57, 58

N

nail clippers forbici per unghie [forbeechee pair lay oongyay] 71

nail file limetta per le unghie [leemetta pair lay oongyay] 71

nail polish smalto per unghie [zmalto pair lay oongyay] 71

nail polish remover acetone per smalto delle unghie [achetonay pair zmalto dellay oongyay] 71

nail-brush spazzola per le unghie [spatzola pair lay oongyay] 71

naked nudo/-a [noodo/-a]

name nome [nomay] 12, 40

nappies pannolini [pannoleenee] 71

nation stato [stato]

nationality nazionalità [natsyonaleeta] 13

natural fibre fibra naturale [feebra natooralay] 66

nature natura [natoora] 54

nausea nausea [nowzay-a] 72

near vicino/-a [veecheeno/-a]

nearest prossimo/prossima [prosseemo/prosseema]

necessary necessario [nechessareeo]

neckerchief fazzoletto da collo [fatzoletto da kollo] 67

neighbour vicino [veecheeno] 13

nephew nipote [neepotay] 13

never mai [maee]

New Zealand la Nuova Zelanda [nwova tzaylanda]

New Zealander neozelandese [nayotzelandayzay]

new nuovo/-a [nwovo/-a]

news notizie [noteetsyay] 82

newspaper giornale [jornalay] 65

next prossimo/prossima [prosseemo/prosseema]

nice gentile [jenteelay]

niece nipote [neepotay] 13

night notte [nottay] 12, 19

nightshirt camicia da notte [kameecha da nottay] 67

no no [no]

nobody nessuno [nessoono]

noise rumore [roomoray]

noisy rumoroso [roomorozo]

non-smoker non fumatore [non foomatoray] 30, 31

normal normale [normalay]

north nord [nord] 22

not non [non]

notary notaio [notayo] 79

nothing niente [nyentay]

nowhere da nessuna parte [da nessoona partay]

number numero [noomairo] 22, 82

O

obvious chiaro/-a [kyaro/-a]

office ufficio [ooffeecho] 49, 81

often spesso [spesso]

old vecchio [vekkyo]

once una volta [oona volta]

only solo [solo]

open aperto/-a [apairto/-a] 80

opening times orari di apertura [oraree dee apairtoora] 49, 80

optician ottico [otteeko] 69

other altro/altra [altro/altra]

otherwise diversamente [deevairsamentay]

owner proprietario [propree-etaryo]

P

pain scherzo [skairtso]

pains dolori [doloree] 72

pair coppia [koppya] 20

palace palazzo [palatzo] 51

papers documenti [dokoomentee] 21, 79

parasol ombrellone [ombrellonay] 53, 61

parcel pacchetto [pakketto] 81

parents genitori [jeneetoree] 13

park parco [parko] 51

part parte [partay]

passage passaggio [passajjo] 23

passenger passeggiero [passejairo] 30, 31

passport passaporto [passaporto] 21, 79

past passato [passato]

pedestrian pedone [pedonay] 49, 52

people popolo [popolo]

percentage percento [pairchento]

performance presentazione [presentatsyonay] 12, 57

perfume profumo [profoomo] 71

petrol benzina [bendzeena] 24

petrol station distributore [deestreebootoray] 24

photography shop negozio fotografico [negotsyo fotografeeko] 67

picture quadro [**kwa**dro] 50, 69
piece pezzo [**pett**zo] 20
pillow cuscino [koo**shee**no] 38
pity (it's a) peccato [pek**ka**to]
place posto [**pos**to]; luogo [**lwo**go] 22
plain pianura [pya**noo**ra] 54
plant pianta [**pyan**ta] 54, 61
plate piatto [**pyat**to] 43
platform binario [b**ee**naryo] 29
please prego [**pray**go]
poisonous velenoso/-a [vele**no**zo/-a]
police officer poliziotto
 [poleets**yot**to] 79
police polizia [poleet**see**a] 79
politics politica [po**lee**teeka]
poor povero [**po**vero]
port porto [**por**to] 31, 50
porter portiere [por**tyai**ray] 32
possible possibile [pos**see**beelay]
postcard cartolina postale
 [karto**lee**na pos**ta**lay] 81
postcode codice di avviamento postale
 [**ko**deechay dee avvee**a**mento
 pos**ta**lay] 81
post-office ufficio postale [oof**feecho**
 pos**ta**lay] 81
pottery ceramica [chai**ra**meeka] 69
powder talco [**tal**ko] 71
prefix prefisso [pre**fees**so] 82
pregnant incinta [een**cheen**ta] 73
present regalo [re**ga**lo] 69
pretty carino/-a [ka**ree**no/-a]
price prezzo [**pret**zo] 61
priest prete [**pret**tay]
programme programma
 [pro**gram**ma] 82
pub cantina [kan**tee**na] 40
public pubblico [**poob**bleeko]
pullover pullover [**pool**lover] 65
punctual puntuale [poont**wa**lay]
punishment multa [**mool**ta] 79
purse portamonete
 [portamo**nay**tay] 79
pyjamas pigiama [pee**ja**ma]

Q

quality qualità [kwal**ee**ta] 40, 61
quarter quartiere
 [kwar**tyai**ray] 22, 51
question domanda [do**man**da] 16
quiet tranquillo/-a [trank**weel**lo/-a]
quiet(ly) a bassa voce
 [a **bas**sa **vo**chay]

R

radio radio [**rad**yo] 39, 82
rain pioggia [**pyo**jja] 20
raincoat impermeabile
 eempairma**ya**beelay] 65
rape stupro [**stoo**pro] 79
rare raro/-a [**ra**ro/-a]
razor blade lamette da barba
 [la**met**tay da **bar**ba] 71
ready pronto/-a [**pron**to/-a]; finito/-a
 [fee**nee**to/-a]
receipt ricevuta [reeche**voo**ta] 43, 77
reception ricezione [reechets**yo**nay] 32
records dischi [**dees**kee] 61
relative parente [pa**ren**tay] 13
responsible responsabile
 [respon**sa**beelay]
rest riposo [ree**po**zo]; tranquillità
 [trankweel**lee**ta]
restaurant ristorante [reesto**ran**tay] 40
result risultato [reezool**ta**to] 54
rich ricco/-a [**rek**ko/-a]
right (correct) giusto/-a [**joo**sto/-a]
right destra [**des**tra]
risk rischio [**rees**kyo] 23, 54, 80
river fiume [**fyoo**may] 50, 54
riverbank riva [**ree**va] 53
road strada [**stra**da] 22
roadside restaurant posto di ristoro
 [**pos**to dee ree**sto**ro] 32
room sala [**sa**la] 51; spazio [**spats**yo] 51
round rotondo/-a [ro**ton**do/-a]
rubbish spazzatura [spatza**too**ra] 39
rucksack zaino [**tza-ee**no] 54

S

sad triste [**tree**stay]
safe sicuro/-a [see**koo**ro/-a]
safety belt cintura di sicurezza
 [cheen**too**ra dee seekoo**ret**za] 26
sale saldi [**sal**dee] 61
sandals sandali [**san**dalee] 67
sanitary towel pannolino
 [panno**lee**no] 71
satisfied soddisfatto/-a [soddees**fat**to/-a]
Saturday sabato [**sa**bato] 17
saucepan pentola [**pen**tola] 39
scheduled flight volo di linea
 [volo dee **lee**nay-a] 30
scissors forbici [**for**beechee] 71
Scotland la Scozia [**skots**ya]
Scottish scozzese [skots**ay**zay]
sea mare [**ma**ray] 53

seafood frutti di mare
[**froot**tee dee **ma**ray] 45
seasickness mal di mare
[mal dee **ma**ray] 31, 72
season stagione [sta**jo**nay] 17;
(high/low) season (alta/fuori)
stagione [(alta/**fwo**ree) sta**jo**nay] 17
seat posto a sedere
[**pos**to a se**dair**ay] 28, 40
sea-urchin riccio di mare
[**reec**ho dee **ma**ray] 53, 72
second secondo [se**kon**do] 19
self-service autoservizio
[owtosair**veet**syo] 40, 61
separate diviso/-a [dee**veez**o/-a]
series fila [**fee**la]
serious serio/-a [**sair**eeo/-a]
service personale di servizio
[pairso**nal**ay dee sair**veet**syo] 41, 61
sex sesso [**ses**so]
shaver rasoio elettrico
[ra**zoy**o elet**tree**ko] 67, 71
shawl scialle [**shal**lay] 67
shirt camicia [ka**mee**cha] 65
shoe cream crema per scarpe
[**kray**ma pair **skar**pay] 65
shoe shop calzoleria [kaltsolai**ree**a] 65
shoelaces legaccioli [lega**cho**lee] 65
shoes scarpe [**skar**pay] 65
shop negozio [ne**got**syo] 61
shore riva [**ree**va] 53
short corto [**kor**to]
shorts pantaloncini *(m/Pl)*
[pantalon**chee**nee] 67
shower doccia [**do**cha] 33, 38, 55
shy timido/-a [**tee**meedo/-a]
sick malato/-a [ma**la**to/-a]
side lato [**la**to]
sign insegna [een**sen**ya] 23, 29, 54
signature firma [**feer**ma] 21, 78
signpost indicatore stradale
[eendeeka**to**ray stra**da**lay] 22
silk seta [**say**ta] 66
single celibe *(m)* [**che**leebay]/nubile *(f)*
[**noo**beelay] 14
sister sorella [so**rel**la] 13
sister-in-law cognata [kon**ya**ta] 13
situation situazione [seetooats**yo**nay]
skirt gonna [**gon**na] 65
sleeper car carrozza a cuccette
[kar**rot**za a koo**chet**tay] 29
sleeve manica [**ma**neeka] 65
slim snello/-a [**znel**lo/-a]

slowly lentamente [lenta**men**tay]
small piccolo/-a [**peek**kolo/-a]
smell odore [o**do**ray] 40
smoke *[vb]* fumare [foo**ma**ray] 71
snack spuntino [spoon**tee**no] 40
soap sapone [sa**po**nay] 39
socks calzini [kalt**see**nee] 65
soft morbido/-a [**mor**beedo/-a]
solicitor avvocato [avvo**ka**to] 79;
notaio [**no**tayo] 79
some alcuni [al**koo**nee]
something qualcosa [kwal**ko**za]
son figlio [**feel**yo] 13
sorry! scusi tanto! [**skoo**zee **tan**to] 13
south sud [sood]; meridione
[mairee**dyo**nay] 22
souvenirs ricordini [reekor**dee**nee] 69
special offer offerta speciale
[of**fair**ta spe**cha**lay] 61
special rate tariffa speciale
[ta**reef**fa spe**cha**lay] 30
speciality specialità [spechal**ee**ta] 40
speed velocità [veloche**eta**] 19
spoon cucchiaio [kook**kya**yo] 43
sport sport [sport] 54, 56
sports articles articoli sportivi
[ar**tee**kolee spor**tee**vee] 61
sportsground campo sportivo
[**kam**po spor**tee**vo] 54
spring primavera [preema**vai**ra] 17
spring sorgente [sor**jen**tay] 51, 54
square piazza [**pyat**za] 22, 30, 41, 51
staircase scala [**ska**la] 38
stamp francobollo [franko**bol**lo] 81
starter antipasto [antee**pas**to] 44
station stazione [stats**yo**nay] 29
stationery cartoleria [kartolai**ree**a] 65
stay soggiorno [so**jor**no] 15
steward cameriere di bordo
[kamair**yair**ay dee **bor**do] 30, 31
stewardess hostess [**os**tess] 30, 31
stockings calze [**kalt**say] 67
stone pietra [**pyay**tra]
stopover scalo [**ska**lo] 30
storey piano [**pya**no] 32
storm tempesta [tem**pes**ta] 20, 55;
temporale [tempo**ra**lay] 20
story racconto [rak**kon**to]
straight on dritto [**dreet**to]
street strada [**stra**da] 22
stupid stupido/-a [**stoo**peedo/-a]
subway sottopassaggio
[sottopas**saj**jo] 23

suede camoscio [kamosho] 65, 69
suit (for men) vestito da uomo
  [vesteeto da womo] 67
suit (for women) costume
  [kostoomay]
suitcase valigia [valeeja] 29, 32, 79
summer estate [estatay] 17
sun sole [solay] 20
sunburn scottatura da sole
  [skottatoora da solay] 72, 77
suncream latte solare
  [lattay solaray] 71
Sunday domenica [domeneeka] 17
sunglasses occhiali da sole
  [okkyalee da solay] 70
suntan lotion crema solare
  [krayma solaray] 71
supermarket supermercato
  [soopairmairkato] 61
supper cena [chayna] 34, 40
supplement (for train ticket)
  supplemento [sooplaymento] 29
surprise sorpresa [sorprayza]
sweets dolciumi [dolchoomee]
swimming costume costume da bagno
  per donna
  [kostoomay da banyo pair donna] 67
swimming pool piscina
  [peesheena] 33, 53
swimming trunks costume da bagno
  per uomo
  [kostoomay da banyo pair womo] 67
synthetic material sintetico
  [seenteteeko] 66

T
table tavolo [tavolo] 40
tablets pastiglie [pasteelyay] 73, 77
take-off decollo [dekollo] 30; partenza
  [partentsa] 54
tampons tamponi [tamponee] 71
taste gusto [goosto] 40
telegram telegramma [telegramma] 81
telephone telefono [telayfono] 82
telephone conversation chiamata
  interurbana
  [kyamata eentairoorbana] 82
telephone directory elenco telefonico
  [elenko telefoneeko] 82
temperature temperatura
  [tempairatoora] 20, 73
terminus l'ultima stazione
  [loolteema statsyonay] 28, 29

terrible spaventoso/-a [spaventozo/-a]
thank you grazie [gratsyay] 13
theatre teatro [tayatro] 57
theft furto [foorto] 79
thick grosso/-a [grosso/-a]
thin sottile [sotteelay]
thing cosa [kosa]; oggetto [ojetto]
thirst sete [saytay] 48
through-carriage vagone diretto
  [vagonay deeretto] 29
Thursday giovedì [jovaydee] 17
ticket biglietto [beelyetto] 28, 29, 57
tide mareggiata [marayjata] 31
tie cravatta [kravatta] 67
tights calzamaglia [kaltsamalya] 67
timber legno [laynyo] 37
time tempo [tempo] 17, 19
timetable orario di viaggio
  [oraryo dee vyajjo] 28, 29
tip mancia [mancha] 43, 83
tired stanco/-a [stanko/-a]
tiring faticoso/-a [fateekozo/-a]
tobacco tabacco [tabakko] 71
tobacconist's tabaccheria
  [tabakkairee-a] 71
together insieme [eensyaymay]
toilet paper carta igienica
  [karta eejeneeka] 39, 71
toilet gabinetto [gabeenetto] 39
tomorrow domani [domanee] 17
too much troppo [troppo]
toothbrush spazzolino [spatzoleeno] 71
toothpaste dentifricio
  [denteefreecho] 71
total somma [somma] 43
tourist turista [tooreesta] 21, 49
tourist guide guida turistica [gweeda
  tooreesteeka] 49, 65
tourist office ufficio di informazioni
  turistiche [ooffeecho dee
  eenformatsyonee tooreesteekay] 49
tourist sight monumento
  [monoomento] 52
towel tovagliolo [tovalyolo] 43
tower torre [torray] 51
town città [cheetta] 22, 51
town hall municipio
  [mooneecheepyo] 51
town map carta della città
  [karta della cheetta] 49, 65
toy giocattolo [jokattolo] 61
toyshop negozio di giocattoli
  [negotsyo dee jokattolee] 61

traffic lights semaforo [se**ma**foro] 22
traffic traffico [**traf**feeko] 23
train treno [**tray**no] 29
trainers scarpe da ginnastica
  [**skar**pay da jeen**nas**teeka] 67
tram tram [tram] 28
translator interprete
  [een**tair**pretay] 80
travel agent agenzia di viaggi
  [ajent**see**a dee **vyaj**jee] 49, 52
traveller's check assegno turistico
  [as**sen**yo too**rees**teeko] 33, 78
tree albero [**al**bairo] 54
trip into the country gita campestre
  [**jee**ta kam**pay**stray] 31
trousers pantaloni *(m/Pl)*
  [panta**lo**nee] 65
truck camion [**kam**eeon] 23
true vero/-a [**vair**o/-a]
T-shirt T-Shirt [T-shirt] 65
Tuesday martedì [marta**ay**dee] 17
tunnel tunnel [**toon**nayl] 23
tweezers pinzetta [peent**set**ta] 71
tyre pneumatico [pnayoo**ma**teeko] 26

U

ugly brutto/-a [**broot**to/-a]
umbrella ombrello [om**brel**lo] 61
uncle zio [**tse**eo] 13
underground metropolitana
  [metropolee**tan**a] 28
underpants mutande [moo**tan**day] 67
understand capire [ka**pee**ray]
underwear biancheria intima
  [byankai**ree**a een**tee**ma] 65
unhappy infelice [eenfe**lee**chay]
urgent urgente [oor**jen**tay]

V

valid valido/-a [va**lee**do/-a]
value valore [va**lor**ay]
vegetables verdura [vair**doo**ra] 62
very molto [**mol**to]
vest maglia [**mal**ya] 67
video (cassette) (cassette) video
  [(kas**set**tay) video] 67
view vista [**vee**sta] 50
viewpoint punto di vista
  [**poon**to dee **vee**sta] 50
village paese [pa-**ay**zay] 22, 50
visa visto [**vee**sto] 21
visible visibile [veezee**bee**lay]
visit visita [**vee**zeeta] 49, 52

W

waistcoat gilè [jee**lay**] 67
waiter cameriere [kamair**yair**ay] 41
waiting room sala di attesa
  [sala dee at**tay**za] 72
waitress cameriera [kamair**yair**a] 41
Wales il Galles [**galles**]
walk passeggiata [passay**ja**ta] 49, 54
warm caldo/-a [**kal**do/-a]
warning attenzione [attents**yo**nay] 23
washing powder detergente
  [detair**jen**tay] 71
washing-up liquid detersivo per i
  piatti [detair**see**vo pair ee **pyat**tee]
watchmaker orologiaio [orolo**ja**yo] 66
water acqua [**ak**wa] 37, 39, 48
wave onda [**on**da] 55
weather forecast previsioni del tempo
  [preveez**yo**nee del **taym**po] 20, 82
weather tempo [**tem**po] 20
Wednesday mercoledì [mairkolay**dee**] 17
week settimana [settee**ma**na] 17, 19
weight peso [**payz**o] 19, 61
welcome benvenuto [benve**noo**to]
wellington boots stivale di gomma
  [stee**va**lay dee **gom**ma] 65
Welsh gallese [gallay**zay**]
west ovest [**ov**est] 22
wet bagnato/-a [**ban**yato/-a]
wide largo/-a [**lar**go/-a]
wife moglie [**mol**yay] 13
wind vento [**vent**o] 20
winter inverno [een**vair**no] 17
witness testimone [testee**mo**nay] 25, 79
woman signora [seen**yor**a] 12, 13
wood bosco [**bosk**o] 51, 54
wool lana [**lan**a] 66
word parola [pa**ro**la]
work lavoro [la**vor**o] 14
workshop officina [offee**chee**na] 25, 27
world mondo [**mon**do]
written scritto/-a [**skreet**to/-a]
wrong falso/-a [**fal**so/-a]

Y

year anno [**an**no] 17, 20
yes sì [**see**]
young giovane [**jo**vanay]
youth hostel ostello [o**stel**lo] 38

Z

zip chiusura lampo
  [kyoo**zoo**ra lampo] 61

Italian-English A–Z

A
acqua (non) potabile (not) drinking water
aeroporto airport
albergo hotel
ambulanza ambulance
annuncio display
arrivo arrival
attenzione caution
autogrill motorway services
autostrada motorway

B
banca bank
barbiere gent's hairdresser
benvenuti welcome
benzina petrol
biblioteca library
biglietteria ticket office
binario platform

C
cabina cabin
cabina telefonica telephone box
calzolaio shoemaker
cambio bureau de change
camping camp-site
casello autostradale toll-booth
cassa cash desk
centro centre
chiuso closed
cimitero cemetery
cinema cinema
coda traffic jam
cognome surname
cuccetta sleeper carriage

D
deviazione diversion
distributore petrol station
divieto di sorpasso no overtaking
divieto di transito no through road
donne ladies' toilet

E
edicola kiosk
entrata libera admission free

F
fabbrica factory
famiglia family
fare la fila to queue
farmacia chemist
fatto a mano hand-made
fermata bus-stop
fermo posta poste restante
festivo holiday
freno di emergenza emergency brake
frontiera border
frutta e verdura fruit and vegetables
fumatori smokers

G
gas gas
giornali newspapers
giorni feriali weekdays
girare to turn off

I
importante important
imposta di valore aggiunto (IVA) value added tax
informazioni information

L
lago lake
lettera letter
libero free
libreria bookshop
listino prezzi price list

M
macelleria butcher's
meccanico mechanic
metropolitana underground
mostra exhibition

N
nave boat
nome name
non fumatori non-smokers

O
offerta speciale special offer
ospedale hospital
ottico optician

P
pacco package
panetteria bakery
parcheggio car-park
parrucchiere hairdresser
partenza departure
pedaggio motorway toll
pericolo di morte danger of death
pericoloso danger
pittura fresca wet paint
polizia police
porto port
premere to press
prenotazione reservation
prevendita advance ticket sales
programma programme

R
ricevuta fiscale invoice, bill
riduzione reduction
rifiuti rubbish
ritardo delay

S
sala d'attesa waiting room
salumeria cooked meat shop
scontrino receipt
senso unico one-way street

senza piombo lead-free
signori gentlemen
società society; company
spettacolo presentation
sposato/-a married
spremuta fruit juice
supermercato supermarket

T
tabacchi tobacco goods
teatro theatre
teatro comunale municipal theatre
tirare to pull
trattoria restaurant
tutto compreso everything included

U
ufficio office
ufficio postale post office
urgente urgent
uscita exit, way out

V
via road
vietato fumare no smoking

Photo Credits

All pictures Veit Haak except APA Publications/Frances Gransden: 81; Rainer Hackenberg: 17, 25 (right), 40; Herbert Hartmann: 37; Gerold Jung: 32, 53, 65 (right); Markus Kirchgeßner: 61, 72; Daniele Messina: 77; The Stock Market: cover.